The LAMB *of* GOD

Clarence E. Macartney

Previously Unpublished Sermons by

CLARENCE E. MACARTNEY

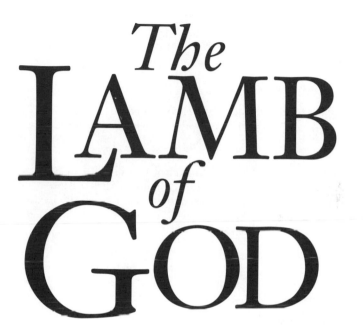

The LAMB *of* GOD

Compiled by

RICHARD ALLEN BODEY

kregel
PUBLICATIONS

Grand Rapids, MI 49501

The Lamb of God: Previously Unpublished Sermons by Clarence E. Macartney compiled by Richard Allen Bodey.

Copyright © 1994 by Richard Allen Bodey.

Published by Kregel Publications, a division of Kregel, Inc., P.O. Box 2607, Grand Rapids, MI 49501. Kregel Publications provides trusted, biblical publications for Christian growth and service. Your comments and suggestions are valued.

Cover and book design: Alan G. Hartman

Library of Congress Cataloging-in-Publication Data
Macartney, Clarence E. (Clarence Edward), 1879–1957.
    The Lamb of God: previously unpublished sermons by Clarence E. Macartney / by Clarence E. Macartney: compiled by Richard Allen Bodey.
        p.   cm.
    1. Atonement—Sermons. 2. Jesus Christ—Person and offices—Sermons. 3. Sermons, American.
4. Presbyterian Church—Sermons. I. Bodey, Richard Allen. II. Title.
BT268.M33   1994   252'.051—dc20   94-23031
                                                                                CIP
ISBN 0-8254-2151-9

    1 2 3 4 5 6 Printing / Year 98 97 96 95 94

Printed in the United States of America

To the memory of John Robertson McCartney, brother of Clarence Edward Macartney, who first invited the editor to prepare this collection of sermons for publication more than thirty-five years ago.

"Fern Cliffe"—Macartney's home at
Geneva College, Beaver Falls, Pennsylvania

Macartney Room,
Geneva College—sketch
by Eric Dugan, '80

Macartney Library
Tower, Geneva
College—sketch by
Patricia Kempton, '85

Contents

PART TWO
The Secret of the Universe

1

Preface

A curious scrap of history underlies the publication of this book, particularly my association with it, which may be of some interest to the reader.

In November 1956, I assumed the pastorate of the Third Presbyterian Church of North Tonawanda, New York, which was preparing to observe its Golden Anniversary the following spring. At my suggestion, the Planning Committee decided to invite Dr. Macartney, one of my favorite homiletical heroes, for the occasion. When I wrote the letter of invitation, I learned that he was dying.

After Dr. Macartney's death, I was asked by Robertson McCartney[1] if I would care to edit an unpublished series of his brother's sermons on "The Lamb of God." I was overjoyed at the prospect, which, in view of my youth (I had graduated from seminary only two years previously),

---

1. Some of the Macartneys spelled the family name "McCartney".

I considered a double honor. When the box containing the original typescripts—with markings and revisions in the author's own handwriting—arrived, I knew at once that these messages deserved a place alongside Dr. Macartney's many volumes of published sermons. For some reason, however, I never carried out the project. I think I became intimidated by my youthful inexperience and unfamiliarity with the publishing world and its demands. In any event, the box collected dust in my study for several years, until I reluctantly returned it.

More than a quarter of a century went by. Then one day I found myself on a committee with Dr. John H. White, then a vice president at Geneva College in Beaver Falls, Pennsylvania. It was at Fern Cliffe, the home on the Geneva campus where Dr. Macartney grew up and where he lived in retirement until his death. I told Dr. White about the long-forgotten project and learned that the sermons were in the Macartney archives at Geneva. He welcomed with enthusiasm my expression of renewed interest in editing the series and graciously volunteered to make the materials available to me. When I subsequently approached Kregel Publications, I was delighted to receive a green light. Thus, by a strange and circuitous route I have, in the good providence of God, come at last to redeem a pledge made more than thirty-five years ago.

Many individual sermons have been preached on "The Lamb of God." Not so common, however, are extended series on this theme. In this collection Dr. Macartney explores the rich vein of truth surrounding this dominant image in the book of Revelation. No less than twenty-eight times John employs this term to describe the glorified Christ. It is instructive to recall that with this very same description the apostle was first introduced to Jesus when he heard his teacher, John the Baptist, exclaim as Jesus passed by, "Look, here is the Lamb of God" (John 1:36 NRSV).[2] So first impressions often become lasting ones.

One sermon in the series, "The Victory of the Lamb," has survived only in extended outline form. To flesh it out would, at best, have been a formidable challenge. When I was working through the Macartney files, I discovered another series of four messages on the theme, "The Blood of Christ." Because of the interrelatedness of the two series, I decided to include the latter one as well. By another happy providence the third sermon in this series, "The Blood of Christ: How It Conquers," covers some of the same terrain as that in "The Victory of the Lamb." I therefore decided not to attempt to reconstruct the latter message but to omit it altogether and thus avoid betraying the work of an imitator's hand.

Although the First Presbyterian Church of Pittsburgh, Pennsylvania, issued these sermons as pamphlets immediately after their delivery, Dr. Macartney never prepared them for formal publication in a book. Here and there I have, for one reason or another, thought it best to make minor editorial changes. In every instance I have preserved the author's meaning and tried to retain his rhetorical style. It should be noted in this connection that Dr. Macartney, like most preachers of his day, quoted biblical passages from the King James Version.

Preachers will find in these pages many fertile ideas for sermons of their own. A preacher who did not object even when others took his sermons lock, stock, and barrel, Dr.

---

2. The Greek word for *lamb* used by the apostle John for Jesus in the book of Revelation is different from the word in the salutation of John the Baptist recorded in the Fourth Gospel. There is no difference in meaning, however, in these passages.

Macartney would certainly rejoice in this extension of his usefulness in the furtherance of the Gospel. But the messages also promise to bestow great spiritual treasures on all who read them. Editor and publisher alike, therefore, hope that they will find their way into the hands and hearts of large numbers of readers beyond the ranks of the clergy. Indeed, may the readers include many who will find in them the means of their own saving encounter with "the Lamb of God who takes away the sin of the world" (John 1:29 NRSV).

I wish to express my profound appreciation to Dr. John H. White, now President of Geneva College; Dr. Gerald D. Moran, the college librarian; and the members of the library staff, who opened the way for me to resume this project and without whose generous assistance I could not have completed it.

I also want to thank Dennis Hillman, Senior Editor of Kregel Publications, and all the others there who also helped to make it possible for me to enjoy the privilege of preparing these messages for publication.

To Ruth, my wife and partner in ministry, for her labor in typing and proofreading, and to Judy Tetour and Wendy Turner of Trinity Evangelical Divinity School, who transferred the material to the computer, I am likewise grateful.

I further acknowledge my indebtedness to the Senate, Administration, and Board of Regents of Trinity Evangelical Divinity School for granting me the sabbatical during which this work was done.

RICHARD ALLEN BODEY

Biographical Sketch

It is obvious, remarked a prominent professor of preaching, that God never intended to save the world through great preaching for throughout the centuries He has given His church few great preachers. Clarence Edward Macartney was one of these few exceptions.

The youngest of seven children—four boys and three girls—he was born in Northwood, Ohio, in 1879, into a home, as he described it, "of plain living and high thinking."[1] His father, John Longfellow Macartney, was pastor of the local Reformed (Covenanter) Presbyterian Church. All four sons followed him into the gospel ministry but left the denomination of their childhood to serve in the much larger (Northern) Presbyterian Church USA. Both

---

1. Henry, J. Clyde, ed. *The Making of a Minister: The Autobiography of Clarence E. Macartney.* Great Neck, NY: Channel Press, 1961, p. 28. I am indebted to this volume for much of the material in this brief sketch of Dr. Macartney's life and ministry.

parents were cultured, loving, and devout, and while both exercised a strong and enduring influence over their children, the mother was the more dominant personality.

Northwood was the home of Geneva College, an institution of the Reformed Presbyterian Church. While he was still at Northwood, Dr. Macartney's father, a man of uncommonly wide general knowledge, was appointed Professor of Natural Science at the college. When Clarence Macartney was only nine months old, the college relocated to Beaver Falls in western Pennsylvania, thirty miles north of Pittsburgh, and the Macartneys moved with it. The family took up residence at Fern Cliffe, a new home built for them on the college campus on a hill overlooking the Beaver River. The spiritual and intellectual atmosphere of the college, with its firm commitment to historic Christian orthodoxy in the Calvinistic tradition, made a lifelong impact upon Dr. Macartney's character and convictions. Throughout his many years of ministry he remained profoundly grateful for that influence. Here, too, as a boy he heard orations and declamations on various occasions and began to acquire the oratorical taste that later became a hallmark of his preaching style. At Fern Cliffe, with his parents and siblings properly seated for his congregation, he made his first attempts at preaching.

The father's failing health led the family to leave Beaver Falls for California, and afterwards Denver, several years before Dr. Macartney entered college. After a year at the University of Denver, he joined his older brother Albert at the University of Wisconsin. Here he distinguished himself in one of the debating societies, and at the end of his junior year represented the university in the Northern Oratorical League Contest, winning second place. After his graduation in 1901, uncertain about his life's work, he traveled abroad for awhile, then returned to Fern Cliffe in Beaver Falls, where his parents were again residing. He later worked for several months as a reporter for the county newspaper. Looking back many years later he wrote, "If in any way my pulpit preaching and my writings have been clear or interesting, I owe much of that to my newspaper experience."[2]

While working for the newspaper, Dr. Macartney decided to prepare for the ministry. His mother, who supported him with her prayers and encouragement, had long felt that this was his destiny. Because his brother Albert was already a student at Princeton Theological Seminary and because of some rebelliousness against the strict orthodoxy on which he had been reared, he set out for Yale Divinity School, where a moderately liberal theology prevailed. He barely landed at Yale, however, when he suddenly changed his mind and, in his words, "retreated to Princeton," a decision he never regretted. At Princeton, then the great citadel of Presbyterian orthodoxy in America, he was reconfirmed in the faith of the Westminster Confession and Catechisms, never to falter again.

He received his training in preaching from Dr. David James Burrell, well-known pastor of the Marble Collegiate Dutch Reformed Church of New York City, who also taught at the seminary. While serving his first summer student pastorate, armed with only two sermons and few books, he drew heavily on the lives of Bible characters for his Sunday sermons. From this experience he learned the powerful appeal of biographical preaching of

---

2. Ibid., p. 118.

which he went on to become one of the masters of his
day.

Not long before his graduation from Princeton in 1905,
Dr. Macartney was called to the pastorate of the prominent
First Presbyterian Church of Paterson, New Jersey, where
his preaching attracted large congregations. In 1914 he
received a call from the Arch Street Presbyterian Church
in Philadelphia. Boasting one of the city's most magnificent edifices and heir of a proud past, the church had fallen
on hard times and the congregation had dwindled severely.
The young preacher accepted the challenge and the church
soon revived. A few years after his arrival it became one of
the pioneers in broadcasting Sunday services over the ra-
dio. In October 1915 he preached his celebrated sermon,
"Come Before Winter," which he delivered every autumn
thereafter to the close of his ministry.

In the early 1920's, Dr. Macartney rose to national
prominence as a leader in the Fundamentalist–Modernist
controversy that shook the Presbyterian denomination to
its foundations, when he launched a counter–attack against
the brilliant liberal preacher, Dr. Harry Emerson Fosdick.
It was in response to Fosdick's widely publicized sermon,
"Shall the Fundamentalists Win?" which he preached from
the pulpit of the First Presbyterian Church of New York
City. Nominated by William Jennings Bryan, Dr.
Macartney was elected Moderator of the General Assembly of the Presbyterian Church in 1924. Also while at
Arch Street Church, he taught preaching classes at
Princeton Seminary and was elected Professor of Chris-
tian Ethics and Apologetics with the intention that he
would subsequently be shifted to the chair of homiletics.
Preferring the pulpit to the classroom, he declined the
appointment.

In 1927 Dr. Macartney became pastor of the First Presbyterian Church of Pittsburgh, Pennsylvania, where he succeeded Dr. Maitland Alexander, grandson of Archibald Alexander, the revered theologian and founder of Princeton Seminary. For more than twenty–six years crowds thronged the huge downtown Gothic church every Sunday morning and evening to hear the impassioned eloquence with which he proclaimed the Word of the living God. In addition to his Sunday sermons, he normally carried three other speaking assignments each week, sometimes more. Yet he faithfully maintained an extensive schedule of pastoral visitation in hospitals and in the homes of his people throughout the city and its suburbs. The church published hundreds of his sermons in pamphlet form, many copies of which literally reached to the ends of the earth.

Dr. Macartney's preaching was always, first and foremost, biblical. His sermons were saturated with Scripture. Two days before his death, he told his brother Robertson, who was leaving for a preaching engagement, "Put all the Bible you can into it."[3] The words could easily have served as the motto for his own pulpit ministry.

His preaching was unashamedly theological. Firmly anchored in his Calvinistic heritage, it resonated with the grand themes of the Christian revelation: the sovereignty of God, the Deity of Christ, the atonement, the resurrection, the return of Christ, the new birth, repentance, justification by faith, divine providence, the preservation of the believer, eternal life. He did not dodge difficult doctrines like suffering, judgment, and hell, but presented them candidly and compassionately.

Geared to life, his sermons were practical, clear in ap-

3. Ibid., p. 18.

plication, and showed a sympathetic understanding of the human heart. He did not hesitate to kindle the emotions of his hearers, always however, in the interests of rousing them to action. Listening to him in the pulpit, one observed the skill of an accomplished physician of the soul and the ability of a persuasive moral and spiritual motivator. Never did he resort to any tricks of psychological manipulation.

He was a master of the art of illustration, drawing generously upon his vast knowledge of history and literature, including notable poetry. Rarely, however, did he use intimate personal illustrations, except from his family home.

His style at times was dramatic, though never theatrical; oratorical, but not ornate; grand, but not grandiloquent. He never played to the galleries, never stooped to affectation. He was genuine through and through. His descriptive powers, especially when portraying biblical scenes and characters, few preachers have surpassed. Frequently a flash of glistening imagery would set his thought aglow in the hearers' minds. I can still recall his description of the witch of Endor's shock when in response to her incantations the deceased prophet Samuel appeared—a sermon I heard him preach when I was a seminary student forty years ago.

His preaching also struck a strong evangelistic accent. Dr. J. Clyde Henry, his associate during the last twelve years of his ministry, says that in nearly every message he preached, Dr. Macartney pointed out the way of salvation.[4]

Although he dictated his sermons to a secretary and often revised them before delivery, he always preached

---

4. Ibid., p. 20.

without notes, a method he strongly advocated in his book *Preaching Without Notes.*

Dr. Macartney frequently preached and lectured at colleges and universities, theological seminaries, and pastors conferences. A prolific author, he contributed to many journals and magazines and published fifty books, including numerous collections of sermons, a study of preachers which he delivered at Princeton Seminary, a time–honored treasury of illustrations, his autobiography, and several volumes on the Civil War, a subject on which he was a recognized authority. Readers of this book will find echoes of that historical interest in several of the sermons.

In recognition of his many accomplishments, he was awarded the honorary D.D. from Geneva College in 1914, the Litt.D. from Geneva College in 1933, and the LL.D. from Washington and Jefferson College in 1939. He served on the Board of Directors of Princeton Theological Seminary and later of Westminster Theological Seminary.

After an extended illness, Dr. Macartney resigned his Pittsburgh pastorate in 1953. Through the generosity of Geneva College he retired to Fern Cliffe, where he labored on his autobiography and prepared other materials for publication until his failing health allowed him to do so no longer. There amid scenes most precious to him and with members of his family at his side, he went home to be with the Lord he so fervently loved and so faithfully served on February 19, 1957, and "all the trumpets sounded for him on the other side."

Clarence E. Macartney in his study

Part One

The Lamb of God

Behold The Lamb Of God!

Behold the Lamb of God!
O thou for sinners slain,
Let it not be in vain
    That thou hast died:
Thee for my Saviour let me take,
My only refuge let me make
    Thy pierced side.
Behold the Lamb of God!
All hail, Incarnate Word,
Thou everlasting Lord,
    Saviour most blest;
Fill us with love that never faints,
Grant us with all thy blessed saints
    Eternal rest.
Behold the Lamb of God!
Worthy is He alone
To sit upon the throne
    Of God above:
One with the Ancient of all days,
One with the Comforter in praise,
    All Light and Love.

Matthew Bridges, 1845

1

The Blood of the Lamb

These are they which came out of great tribulation, and
have washed their robes, and made them white in the
blood of the Lamb. (Revelation 7:14)

In the last great book of the Bible, the book of Revelation,
the Lamb of God is the dominant personality. The Lamb
standing, as though it had been slain, opens the seven–
sealed book of human destiny. The Lamb makes war on
the beast and all the enemies of God. The terror of the
judgment is the wrath of the Lamb. The redeemed church
is the bride of the Lamb. The followers of Christ overcome
Satan through the blood of the Lamb. The ten thousand
times ten thousand in heaven sing their praises to the Lamb
slain from the foundation of the world. The redeemed are
those whose names are written in the Lamb's Book of Life.
Here in this passage from which we take our text the
company of the saved are those who "have washed their
robes, and made them white in the blood of the Lamb."

Here, then, we have the sublime truth of the atonement, what Christ did for us on the cross, and how the blood of the Lamb, that is, Christ, offered for our sins, is the ground of our pardon and forgiveness, how it redeems us from the bondage of sin, reconciles us to God, and cleanses our souls from the stain of sin.

To attempt to speak upon such a vast truth is like launching out on the ocean upon a raft of logs. If even the angels in amazement desire to look into it, what shall the intellect of man do with it? Even the cherubim and the seraphim bow before it, veiling their faces. The best we can do is to touch the hem of its crimson robe. But in this truth is the length and the breadth and the depth and the height of the Christian faith.

The Lamb of God as He always appears in the Bible is the Son of God, our Redeemer. That was the first salutation given to Christ by man: "Behold the Lamb of God, which taketh away the sin of the world." When Philip preached to the Ethiopian eunuch, he told him that the Lamb spoken of by Isaiah, who was "wounded for our transgressions" and was "dumb before the shearers" is Christ. And the apostle Peter declared that Christ is the Lamb without blemish and without spot.

When the Bible speaks, as it does here through the Communion Service of the blood of Christ, "This cup is the New Testament in my blood," what it means by the blood is the life of Christ offered for our sins. Why did we need such an offering and such a salvation? Because of the fact of sin. Why did God let man sin? That is one of the things that are hid. But the shadow of sin is everywhere. The sun never sets on its ravages. The effects of sin are pollution and guilt. To this fact, conscience and a thousand altars and rites bear witness.

What ought God to have done about sin? He might have destroyed the human race, annihilated it, and thus put an end to sin. That would have been just. But that was not God's purpose in creation. On the other hand, God could not ignore or overlook sin. An infinitely holy God could not do that, for He is "of purer eyes than to behold iniquity." Neither could He just pardon sin without any repentance on the part of the sinner or without any satisfaction for the broken law. Instead of that, God provided full forgiveness and pardon in a way that honors His justice and holiness. Sin was God's problem, and He solved it like a God. He solved it in the mercy and justice and majesty of the atonement, whereby Christ died, "the just for the unjust, that He might bring us to God." So God remains just, and yet the justifier of those who believe in Jesus.

III. The Blood of Christ Justifies Us

Here is one of the great scriptural statements about the power of the Cross and the blood of the Lamb. The thought is that sin breaks the law of God and therefore demands a penalty. The Bible tells us that we have all broken the law of God, that we have all sinned and come short of the glory of God. God, therefore, must deal with sin. His way to deal with it and to make the sinner just in His sight was through the death of Christ. Christ both assumed our guilt and bore our punishment. Literally, He died for us, that is, in our place. Man, therefore, is not merely pardoned and forgiven, but he is also made righteous.

In Germany, there is a church with a lamb cut in the stone over the entrance. This is the story of that lamb. A man working on the steeple of the church lost his footing and fell to the churchyard below. But his fall was broken and his life saved because he fell on a lamb grazing on the grass. So are we saved by the death of the Lamb of God. As Robert Robinson says in his classic hymn, "Come, Thou Fount of Every Blessing,"

> He, to rescue me from danger,
> Interposed His precious blood.

II. THE BLOOD OF CHRIST REDEEMS US

That is another thing the Bible tells us about the power of the Cross. One of the best–loved names of Jesus is the Redeemer. Here the thought is of humanity in the bondage and slavery of sin. The word "redeem" is one that must be explained and interpreted today. It needed no interpretation or explanation in the days of Jesus and the apostles. But the very influence of Christ upon the world has so changed the world that it is necessary to explain the word "redeem." Then the world was half slave. It was common for men to be redeemed from slavery with gold or silver or precious stones. That is the idea back of this beautiful word "redeemer." The precious blood of Christ was the price paid for our redemption. Jesus said that He came to lay down His life as a ransom, a redemption, for many. The apostle Peter said that we have not been redeemed "with corruptible things, as silver and gold, . . . but with the precious blood of Christ, as of a lamb without blemish and without spot." Nothing else, and nothing less, than that great price could have ransomed us.

He only could unlock the gate
Of heav'n, and let us in.

Every believer in Jesus has an obligation to Him and to His church. We have no right to say, "No," to the demands of Christian service. St. Paul gave us the reason when he said, "You are not your own. You have been bought with a price."

III. THE BLOOD OF CHRIST RECONCILES US

"Reconciliation" carries with it the thought of separation and alienation. "Your iniquities," said the prophet Isaiah, "have separated between you and your God, and your sins have hid his face from you, that He will not hear." We know how even in human relationships between one person and another, wrongdoing brings separation, estrangement, and alienation. This is the inevitable effect, even where sin has been hid and covered up. Sin always drives us out: out from our true selves, out from our fellow-human beings, and most of all, out from our God.

How, then, can we be reconciled to God? Not by repentance alone, although that is a part of it, but by the work of Christ on the cross, by the Atonement, which means simply reconciliation, making two people who have been separated to be *at one* again. Even in human relationships there is no nobler or more beautiful work than that of the peacemaker and the reconciler. Martin Luther died in 1546 at Eisleben, where he was born, at the end of an errand of reconciliation. John Bunyan took his last illness on a trip to Reading, where he had gone to reconcile a father and son. It is not strange, then, that God's noblest work is the work of reconciliation. "God was in Christ, reconciling the world unto himself." Hence, the eternal message of the preacher of Christ's church is, as Paul put it, "We pray you in Christ's stead, be ye reconciled to God."

IV. THE BLOOD OF CHRIST CLEANSES US

Here is the eternal paradox for blood is always the special, particular, and unmistakable sign and trace of guilt. What the evildoer is most anxious about is that that stain should be hid and covered. But here we have the divine paradox where blood is not the sign and evidence of guilt, for the precious blood of Christ cleanses and washes the sin-stained soul. That, perhaps, to a truly penitent heart is the worst thing, the thing that he or she feels most about sin—its stain and defilement. The most wonderful thing, the most beautiful thing in the universe, is an immortal soul made in the image of God. Yet that most beautiful and most wonderful thing has upon it the crimson stain of sin.

Here, then, is the wonder-working power of the blood of Christ. It can cleanse us from the stain of sin. So that disciple whom Jesus loved, who leaned upon His breast at the Last Supper, and who impresses us as perhaps the most removed from the stain and penalty of sin of all the apostles, yet he also confessed that he was a sinner. "If we confess our sins, he is faithful and just to forgive us our sins, and to cleanse us from all unrighteousness." Again, he said, "The blood of Jesus Christ his Son cleanseth us from all sin." And here in this great passage from the Apocalypse, the redeemed who stand in the presence of God are described as those who have "washed their robes, and made them white in the blood of the Lamb. Therefore are they before the throne of God." That is, their only ground for standing before the throne of God and of acceptance by Him was that they had washed their robes and made them white in the blood of the Lamb. John goes on to say that they "serve him day and night in his temple and that he that sitteth on the throne shall dwell among them. They shall hunger no more, neither thirst any more; neither shall the sun light on them, nor any heat. For the Lamb which is in the midst of the throne shall feed them and shall lead them unto living fountains of waters, and God shall wipe away all tears from their eyes."

One of the most attractive and honored soldiers of the Confederacy was John Pelham, one of the few junior officers ever commended by General Lee in his reports. He fell in 1863, at the battle of Brandy Station, and his body was carried back to his Alabama home. It was night, and the fields and the vines on the porch of the mansion where he had been born were white in the moonlight. His mother was standing at the door as they bore him in. Looking down on his body, she said through her tears, "Washed white in the blood of the Lamb."

Christiana Rossetti has a moving poem, "Despised and Rejected." A man made fast his door so that false and hollow friends could trouble him no more. But in the night he heard someone knocking at the door and saying to him, "Open, unto me, for my feet bleed. Open thy door and comfort me." But the man within ordered him to go on his way, or he would rise and drive him from his door. The one outside still pleaded with the man within, "Open, and see who stands to plead with thee, lest I should pass thee by, and I one day be as deaf as thou art now."

But again the man within ordered him from his door. All through the night he heard the pleading voice, "Open to me! Rise! Let me in! Open to me that I may come to thee. See my hands bleed that bring thee grace; my heart doth bleed for thee." When the break of day came the voice died away in silence. Then the man within heard footsteps, lingering footsteps, echoing like a sigh, and yet which passed him by. When he opened the door in the morning he saw upon the grass footprints of the night visitor, marked in blood, and lo, on his door was the mark of blood forevermore.

Thus Rossetti describes the sorrow and tragedy of a soul refusing Christ and His redeeming blood. Will the mark of blood be on your door? Or will the precious blood of Christ be your pardon, your reconciliation, your redemption, your cleansing, so that you can join the company and join the song of those who have washed their robes and made them white in the blood of the Lamb?

One of the greatest of the Scottish paraphrases, often sung by a past generation of believers, is the paraphrase of this great verse from the Apocalypse:

> How bright these glorious spirits shine!
> Whence all their white array?
> How came they to the blissful seats
> Of everlasting day?
>
> Lo! these are they from suff'rings great
> Who came to realms of light,
> And in the blood of Christ have washed
> Those robes which shine so bright.

2

The Lamb and the Book

Thou art worthy to take the book, and to open the seals thereof: for thou wast slain . . . (Revelation 5:19)

St. John was now an old man and a prisoner at Patmos for the witness of Christ. His company had gone before. The Gospel which he and his companions had preached apparently had had little effect on that hard, pagan Roman world. Now at the close of his life, like a brilliant sunset at the close of a stormy day, comes the light of this great vision when a window was opened for him into heaven, and he beheld the triumph of the gospel that he had preached and the Christ on whose bosom he had leaned at the Last Supper.

Rising above a sea of glass, John saw a throne set in heaven. Round about the throne were the four and twenty elders and the living creatures with crowns of gold on their heads. Out of the throne proceeded lightnings and thunderings and voices. Around the throne was a rainbow like an emerald and on the throne was the Divine Majesty. In His right hand, He held a seven–sealed book. A strong angel cried with a loud voice, "Who is worthy to open the book, and to loose the seals thereof?" But no one in heaven or on earth was found who was able to open the book or even to look on it. John wept much because none could open the book or even to look on it. But one of the elders comforted him saying, "Weep not; behold the Lion of the tribe of Judah, the Root of David, hath prevailed to open the book and to loose the seven seals thereof."

When John looked again, he saw in the midst of the throne a Lamb standing as though it had been slain. The Lamb came and took the book out of the right hand of Him who sat upon the throne. When He did this all heaven and earth joined in the song, "Thou art worthy to take the book, and to open the seals thereof, for thou wast slain, and hast redeemed us to God by thy blood out of every kindred, and tongue, and people, and nation; and hast made us unto our God kings and priests; and we shall reign on the earth."

Then came the breaking of the seven seals. The Lamb opened the first seal, and behold, a white horse and his rider with a bow and a crown, and he went forth conquering and to conquer. The Lamb opened the second seal, and the red horse, with his rider armed with a great sword, went forth to take peace from the earth. The third seal was opened, and behold, a black horse and his rider, with a pair of balances in his hand, the symbol of famine. The fourth seal was opened, and behold, a pale horse, with

Death for his rider Hell following after him, and power was given him to kill with the sword. The fifth seal was broken, and the souls of those who had been slain for the word of God cried from under the altar. The sixth seal was broken, and there was a great earthquake. The sun became as sackcloth, the moon became as blood, and the stars of heaven fell upon the earth. Men called to the mountains and rocks, "Fall on us, and hide us from the face of him which sitteth upon the throne, and from the wrath of the Lamb."

Then the Lamb opened the seventh seal, and there was silence for the space of half an hour. No songs of the redeemed, no thunders of judgment and doom, but silence in heaven and upon earth. Then the seven angels sounded their trumpets. In quick succession followed wonders and signs and convulsions in heaven and on earth. The infernal powers swarmed out of their dens to assail mankind and make war on the church of God. Then the seventh angel sounded, and great voices were heard in heaven saying, "The kingdoms of this world are become the kingdoms of our Lord, and of his Christ, and he shall reign forever and ever."

That is the great end toward which the world is moving. That is the final answer to the Lord's Prayer, "Thy kingdom come." The kingdom *has* come, and the kingdoms of this world have become the kingdoms of our Lord and his Christ. The seven–sealed book that the Lamb opened contained the history and destiny of mankind and the church. The interpretation, the key, to that history is Christ and Him crucified. The Lamb of God reigns from the cross.

I. CHRIST IS THE KEY TO THE BOOK OF DIVINE REVELATION

What is the Bible? One might answer, "Sixty-six books written by thirty and more authors—some of them educated men, others herdsmen, tax gatherers, and fishermen—through a millennium and a half of time. And in the book, one finds all forms of writing: narrative, biography, codes of law, predictions, soliloquies, dramas, odes, hymns, proverbs. But taken so, the Bible is just a strange jumble and collection of books, a heterogeneous gathering together of aspirations, longings, miracles, prodigies, histories, predictions, but with no clue to the meaning and purpose of it.

The key to the meaning of the Bible is Christ. "These," He said, "are they which testify of me." The Bible is like the Holy City—the Lamb is the light thereof. Put together in the same volume, Leviticus and St. John, Genesis and Revelation, Judges and the Acts of the Apostles, the Psalms and Jude, would seem to be an offense against all ideas of literary unity and consistency. But when once the Cross of Christ lights up these pages, the Bible becomes a wonderful unity, as fixed and sure and beautiful as the stars in heaven. Then can we say:

> My soul rejoices to pursue
> The steps of Him I love;
> Till glory breaks upon my view
> In brighter worlds above.

Without Christ, without the light of the Lamb of God to illuminate it, the Bible is like a great cathedral wrapped in the darkness of night. But with Christ as its interpreter, its Alpha and Omega, the Bible is like a cathedral when the light of the morning sun brings out all its splendor: its massive walls, nave, choir, transepts, soaring arches, windows flaming with the faces of the goodly fellowship of the prophets, the glorious company of the apostles, and the noble army of the martyrs.

II. The Lamb Is the Key to the History of the World

No man or angel was able to look upon the seven-sealed book. Human intelligence and experience can hardly bear to look upon the deep mystery of the world's history. We can record some of the acts and facts of the past, but who can give a meaning and purpose to it all? Who can see good coming out of evil, the final overthrow of wickedness, and the triumph of righteousness?

We must shade our eyes when we attempt to read the pages of this world's history. What a labyrinth! What a tangle! What a confusion! What eruptions and convulsions! What conflict between good and evil, Michael and the Devil ever disputing over the body of Moses! What crucifying and execrating and overwhelming of the good by the cruel, the monstrous, the unjust, the wicked! Yet at the same time, there is the constant resurrection of the ideal of righteousness and truth, the crushing of truth to the earth and it yet ever rising again. What fearful outbreaks of war and destruction and savagery among mankind, each heralded by contemporaries as the worst; yet the next when it comes is always worse than the last! Who can bear to look upon the book of human history? Looking upon its pages one would be tempted to say with the German philosopher, "If God made the world, I should not like to be in the place of God. Its woes would break my heart."

The only key to this strange book of the past and the hidden book of the future is Christ, the Lamb who was slain, and yet who is clothed with power and authority and who sits upon the throne of the universe.

In one of the darkest periods of the Civil War, Harriet Beecher Stowe was seen by one of her sons reading the Bible with a candle in one hand and a crucifix in the other. Asked why she did this, she replied, "Because it is a visible, tangible emblem of my crucified Lord, and it helps me to cling to Him." It is only when we read history and the present and the future in the light of the Cross—the emblem of the divine sorrow and suffering, yet His triumphant purpose—that we can have faith in the goodness and wisdom and power of God.

When John wrote this great vision, the world was dark and hopeless, except where the lamp of faith burned in the heart of the followers of the Lamb. Everywhere the sea of iniquity, licentiousness, and persecution was casting up its mire and dirt. But because he had seen the Lamb of God standing in the midst of the throne, John was able to lift up his eyes from that yellow wave-washed rock in the Aegean and behold the triumph of the Lamb of God. "There was silence in heaven," the silence of acquiescence and wonder at the divine plan. "Just and true in thy ways, thou King of Saints." Now we "know in part." We are like one who is led blindfolded through the camp of God. But we know that God is in the camp, and that Christ goes forth conquering and to conquer.

> In the cross of Christ I glory,
> Towering o'er the wrecks of time;
> All the light of sacred story
> Gathers round its head sublime.

III. THE BOOK OF OUR PERSONAL DESTINY

The world has its history and its problems. But each one of us is a world in one's self, and that world is full of mystery. Of ourselves, we cannot break its seven seals or even look upon it. Indeed, there is much in the way of transgression and sin and error and failure that we do not care to look upon. There is much more of silent suffering, the mental anguish of broken hopes that we do not dare to look upon. In some of the things that have happened we can see great good, but how much there seems to be that is needless, fruitless—mistakes of judgment and not of evil intent or desire; the failure of honest efforts; the limitations of disease and poverty that "chilled the noble currents of the soul"; the aspirations after the best, yet so often the doing of the worst; the taking away of friends and loved ones whose presence warmed and softened the heart, cleared the mind and nerved the arm of endeavor. O seven–sealed book of mystery! Who can break your seals, look upon your page, and read the meaning and the purpose of God?

But, thanks be to God, there is One who can open the book for us. The Lamb of God takes the book out of our hand and opens its seals. To Him we leave the end, confident that what guides us and confronts us and awaits us is not blind chance or fatal necessity, but seeking, wounded, suffering, patient, unfaltering love. "We know we cannot drift beyond this love and care."

In Turgenev's *Fathers and Sons*, which is filled with so much that is tragic and inexplicable, Pavel Petrovitch presented the princess, who had loved him and then forsaken him, with a beautiful ring. Upon it was engraved the Sphinx, signifying that in this hour of grief and disappointment, life to him was an enigma and that to all our prayers and cries and entreaties life is as silent and mysterious and unanswering as the Sphinx. After the death of the princess, Pavel received the ring back. Over the Sphinx on the stone she had cut in rude lines a cross, signifying that the final solution of life's mystery and enigma is the Cross and the divine love that suffered there.

Bring, then, the book of your life to the Lamb of God. He who died on the cross for you will open its pages and tell you its meaning. He will give you faith to wait and faith to hope.

> O Cross, that liftest up my head,
> I dare not ask to fly from thee;
> I lay in dust life's glory dead,
> And from the ground there blossoms red
> Life that shall endless be.

3

The War of the Lamb

These shall make war with the Lamb, and the Lamb
shall overcome them.   (Revelation 17:14)

Henry Martyn, the famous missionary to India and
Persia, once had a debate with a learned Persian as
to the comparative merits of Christianity and Islam. The
Persian scoffed at the lamb as a symbol of Christianity.
What was a lamb compared with a lion! When we read
here in the Apocalypse about the war of the Lamb, we
may wonder at first how a lamb, the symbol of gentleness
and innocence, could make war and that with an adversary
which is a beast. Here is one of the sublime paradoxes of
the Bible. The Lamb conquers the beast. Both are
desperately wounded: the beast with its death-stroke, the
Lamb as if it had been slain. Yet the Lamb emerges as the
victor, and the reason given is that the Lamb is the King
of Kings and the Lord of Lord.

The Atonement or the great work of Christ on the

41

cross, has three references: the first, personal, to me a
sinner; the second to the church; and the third to the
kingdom of evil, predicting its judgment and overthrow.
It is with this third reference that we shall deal today.
The war of the Lamb tells us that the final effect of the
Atonement of Christ is not only the winning of forgiveness and righteousness for sinners, but also the destruction
of evil throughout the universe and the pulling down of
every stronghold of Satan. When Jesus cried out on the
cross, "It is finished!" Satan's empire fell. The Lamb of
God who was led as a sheep to the slaughter emerged
victorious over all the powers of darkness. The Cross is
thus the announcement of a new heaven and a new earth.

I. THE CROSS AND THE VISION OF THE FUTURE

It is from the elevation of the cross that we can survey
the future and behold the conquest of righteousness and
truth. No other mountain is high enough for that vision.
Sinai, the mountain of the law, is not high enough.
Parnassus, with its culture, is not high enough. Olympus
with its gods is not high enough. Only from Calvary can
we command this view of final victory.

Ancient histories told wonderful narratives. In their
analysis of character, as we have it in Plutarch's *Lives*
and in the writings of Thucydides and Herodotus, they
are without a peer. But they had no vision of a great
end, no clue to the great goal of history, no theory of a
power beyond ourselves working for righteousness, no
idea of one increasing purpose running through the ages.
Only the Bible has that. This note is struck at the very
beginning of the Bible where the promise is given that
the seed of the woman shall bruise the head of the ser-

pent. This prediction and expectation reaches its climax in the last book of the Bible, where we behold the triumphant Lamb standing upon Mount Zion, while the empire of sin and evil goes down in tremendous, irrevocable judgment and ruin.

In this view of the end of history, there is great tonic and refreshment for our souls. The aged John was a prisoner on Patmos for the sake of Christ. The world everywhere was hostile to God and to the Gospel. There was no champion able to stand up against the beast who had slain the Lord's disciples and apostles and had chained John to that lonely yellow rock. Within the church, corruption and false doctrine had already appeared. Whichever way John looked from his wave-washed prison, all that he could behold was the monotonous stretches and waste of the sea. Perhaps this is one reason why when he came to describe heaven he said of it, "There shall be no more sea." Whichever way John looked over the world, he saw the sea of iniquity, unable to rest, and ever casting up its mire and dirt. But when this door was opened for him into heaven, he beheld the triumph of the Lamb of God.

If that vision was necessary for the inspiration and encouragement of the church then, it is much more so today, when the church is nineteen hundred years old, instead of a half a century; when there is an increasing tendency to compromise with the world; when the line that divides the church from the world becomes more and more difficult to discern; when Satan has assumed new and more subtle disguises than ever before; and when great sections of humanity are given over to believe a lie. Today, more than ever, we need to see what John saw in Patmos: the beast, the symbol of all the powers of iniquity, going down in battle before the Lamb of God.

II. THE ENEMIES OF THE LAMB

One need not attempt to be certain or dogmatic as to
the particular identification of these persons, characters,
and powers that appear in the Apocalypse. But no one can
be mistaken as to their general significance, for they clearly
represent the powers of darkness.

The first adversary of the Lamb is spoken of as the
beast. It emerges out of the sea as a leopard, a bear, and a
lion—a fearful composite of cruel and brutal power. One
of its seven heads is wounded, as if to death. But its death-
stroke is healed, and it goes forth to deceive the world,
which wonders after it and says, "Who is like the beast?"
It blasphemes God and His church and His name, and
makes war on the followers of Christ.

Vain efforts have been made through the ages to iden-
tify the beast, to confine it to one age, one person, or
one evil institution. Some thought it was Nero; some
pagan Rome; others papal Rome; and some Mohammed.
But the beast is more powerful and more sinister than
any one of these institutions or persons. It is the personification of evil and unbelief in the world. It is as
eternal as human history. Wherever the true church
arises, there the beast arises to oppose it. In this vision it
received what appeared to be a death-stroke, but when it
emerged from the abyss, lo, its death-stroke was healed.
What a picture that is of the persistence of evil in the
world! Driven out in one form and in one institution,
evil comes back again with its death-stroke healed. The
beast is the eternal companion of man. It hides, spouting
blood, for a generation or two. Then it emerges with
new vigor and new subtlety, with a new mask over its
countenance and with new power to deceive. It is the

implacable foe of God and humanity. But in the climax of its rage and development, in its last emergence and its final eruption to make war on the Lamb of God, the beast is overcome by the Lamb. With the devil and the false prophet, it is cast into the lake of fire and brimstone. Sin, the great invader and intruder and destroyer, is driven out of the empire of God. "These shall make war with the Lamb, and the Lamb shall overcome them." The Lamb stands triumphant on Mount Zion. He overcomes with His wounds. He conquers from the cross.

The ally of the beast in this war against the Lamb of God is described as a scarlet woman who rides upon the beast. She is arrayed in scarlet and decked with gold and precious stones and pearls. In her hand is a golden cup full of abomination and filthiness, and she is drunken with the blood of the martyrs of Jesus.

Here, again, this powerful symbol, this scarlet woman, is more than any particular personality or system or institution in any one age or period. She is the personification and symbol of a corrupt and degenerate religion. She rides upon the beast, a powerful parable of how a false church puts itself in alliance with the unbelief and the sins of the world.

Such, then, is the dreadful confederation, the enemy that makes war on the Lamb of God. The most dangerous and most powerful foe of Christianity is not the world in itself, but the world in alliance with false religion. Not evil alone, but evil that penetrates good doctrines and good institutions. Not stark atheism, but atheism that employs the language of faith.

Just as in the conflict pictured by St. John, the odds today seem to be against the Lamb of God and against evangelical Christianity. Everywhere we can discern the denial or the subtle explaining a way under the guise of reinterpretation or the quiet suppression of the cardinal, particular truths that make up the Christian Gospel: sin, judgment, atonement, and pardon. Yet we take courage when we see what the issue was of the war between the beast and its allies and the Lamb of God.

Look at the past. To the Greeks the Gospel was foolishness. To the Jews it was a stumbling block. The pagan Roman empire tried to drown the church in its own blood. The church was assailed from within by corruption and schism. From every consideration, from the viewpoint of both experience and history, the church ought to have withered and died. The religion which centers around the Cross of Christ ought to have disappeared. Yet that has never taken place. In every age and among every race, the Lamb of God, Christ as the Redeemer from sin, has been saluted and acclaimed by the company of true believers. Always, out of the apocalyptic ruins and the apparent wreckage of battlefields lost, it seemed, for Christ and truth, there has emerged, dauntless, unshaken, and invincible, the true religion. Today, throughout the whole world, men and women follow and obey the Lamb of God and crown Him with many crowns.

Therefore, we take great confidence for the future. In one way the atonement of Christ appears to be the weakness of Christ—the failure, rather than the triumph, of God. There He hangs, naked, crowned with thorns, derided, mocked, forsaken. Yet He is the only conqueror. His cross is the power of God for the salvation of the world and for the judgment and overthrow of evil. When the Lamb of God was wounded on Calvary's tree, the powers of darkness received their sentence and Satan received his death-stroke.

The last and only conqueror is Christ. In the gallery of Antoine Wertz at Brussels, you can see the most astounding and overwhelming paintings that you will see anywhere in the world. Most of them expose the brutality and horror of war, but some of them herald the empire of peace and the triumph of Christ. Walking down the hall where these paintings hang, one is suddenly brought to a halt by a great painting that shows Napoleon in hell surrounded by the seried ranks of the slain in battle, together with the widows and orphans of those sacrificed to his ambitions. But a little further along are two more great canvasses. One is entitled, "One of Earth's Great Ones." It is a terrific indictment of man's worship of the warrior and shows a monstrous, colossal giant crushing the bones of men and trampling them under his feet as he cruelly leers upon them.

The other is the "Triumph of Christ." On the cross hangs the Redeemer of the world. It is one of the most beautiful bodies of Christ to be seen in any gallery anywhere. From the points of the crown of thorns streams indescribable light. Great angels are sounding their trumpets, while dark, sinister, and evil figures flee away into the darkness. So at length will it be. The Lamb will overcome all His enemies. Christ is the Last Conqueror! The Light of the World will banish the darkness of the world! Divine Love will conquer sin, and the whole earth will be filled with the knowledge of the glory of the Lord as the waters cover the sea.

4

The Lamb's Book of Life

Names . . . written in the book of life of the Lamb slain from the foundation of the world. (Revelation 13:8)

The most sacramental spot in America is Gettysburg. The natural beauty of that fair, rolling agricultural country with its meadows and winding streams and wooded hills has been embellished by hundreds of monuments and memorials to armies, corps, divisions, brigades, regiments, and companies. There, too, are the statues of generals, officers, and privates. The two most imposing monuments are those of Virginia and Pennsylvania. The Virginia monument commemorates the Confederate Commander, Robert E. Lee. It stands on Seminary Ridge and depicts that great soldier looking out across the rising slope over which Pickett's division made its ill-fated charge

on the third day of the battle. Across the fields on
Cemetery Ridge is the great Pennsylvania monument with
its four great arches and the magnificent dome,
surmounted by an angel with a sword in his hand. Inscribed
on bronze tablets are the names of every Pennsylvania
soldier who fought, or was ready to fight, at Gettysburg.
The sons and daughters, grandsons and granddaughters,
and now even the great-grandsons and great-
granddaughters of those thousands of men, when they go
to Gettysburg, visit the Pennsylvania monument and read
with justifiable pride the names of their ancestors who
fought on that decisive field of human history.

How long will that beautiful monument stand? Who
can tell? The tooth of time has cut down the great monuments of the past. There is no reason to expect that it
will spare that great monument. It is not beyond the
reach of imagination to think of the day when that beautiful and sacramental field will become a great desolation.
We can, indeed, envision the day when that Pennsylvania monument and the hundreds of the others will lie
broken, fallen, and laid low, covered with debris. Perhaps, as with the fate of so many of the great memorials
of past ages, their stone and marble will be turned into a
quarry for the erection of new buildings. The antiquar-
ian of a future age may wander amid that desolation and
wonder what these broken stones were and whose worship or deeds or conquests they commemorated. The
day will come when no one will be able to read a single
one of those thousands of names on Pennsylvania's great
monument at Gettysburg.

There is only one tablet, one monument, one book,
where names are inscribed forever. That is the Book of
Life of the Lamb slain from the foundation of the world.

I. THE BOOK OF LIFE IN THE BIBLE

The Book of Life is a favorite figure or symbol in the Bible to describe those who are accepted by God and belong to the company of the redeemed. The book of Exodus tells how the people of Israel rebelled and worshipped a golden calf while Moses was absent on Mount Sinai. When he came down from the mount, Moses assembled the people according to their tribes and families and told them that they had committed a great sin, but that he would go to the Lord and make an atonement for their sin. In his prayer to God, Moses pleaded, "Oh, this people have sinned a great sin, and have made them gods of gold. Yet now, if thou wilt forgive their sin—; and if not, blot me, I pray thee, out of thy book which thou hast written." In his noble intercession Moses, moved with compassion for the guilty people, pleads with God to pardon them. But if God will not do it, then let Him blot Moses' own name out of the Book of Life. What he meant, no doubt, was that he offered himself as an atonement for the people and was willing to have his name blotted out, to have no inheritance in the Land of Canaan, if on that condition God would spare the people.

The Book of Malachi, the last book of the Old Testament, tells us that in the midst of great apostasy and unbelief among God's people, there were still those who feared the Lord and obeyed His commandments and thought upon His name. "Then they that feared the Lord spake often one to another, and the Lord hearkened, and heard it, and a book of remembrance was written before him for them that feared the Lord, and that thought upon his name. 'And they shall be mine,' saith the Lord of Hosts, 'in that day when I make up my jewels, and I will spare them, as a man spareth his own son that serveth him.'" Here, again, we have the figure of a book in which are inscribed the names of those who belong to God.

When the Seventy returned to Christ after their first expedition of preaching and healing and rejoiced greatly because the devils were subject unto them in the name of Christ, Jesus also rejoiced with them and said, "I beheld Satan as lightning fall from heaven. . . . Notwithstanding in this rejoice not, that the spirits are subject unto you, but rather rejoice because your names are written in heaven."

Likewise, St. Paul writing to his friends in the church at Philippi, the best loved of his churches, entreats them— or one of them in particular, possibly St. Luke or Epaphroditus—to "help those women which labored with me in the gospel, with Clement also, and other of my fellow laborers, whose names are in the Book of Life." Paul mentions only one of those names, "Clement." He does not feel it necessary to mention the others because their names are all written before God in the Book of Life, and if they are faithful to Christ, their names will shine out hereafter as the stars forever and ever when the greatest names of time have faded into oblivion.

In the great passage of the twelfth chapter of Hebrews, the author, contrasting the fear and terror of the people when the law was given at Sinai, says that Christian believers, instead of coming to that terrible Mount, have "come unto Mt. Sion and unto the city of the living God, the heavenly Jerusalem, and to an innumerable company of angels, to the general assembly and church of the first-born, which are written in heaven, and to God the Judge of all, and to the spirits of just men made perfect, and to Jesus the Mediator of the new covenant." The whole company of the redeemed have their names inscribed, as it were, in a book of remembrance of life.

When we come to the last book of the Bible, the book of Revelation, we find that the Book of Life, especially the Lamb's Book of Life, is a favorite figure and symbol. In the letter to the church at Sardis, one of the most unworthy of the seven churches mentioned here, yet a church which had a few names, "even in Sardis," which had not defiled their garments and had been faithful to Christ—Christ gives the promise, "He that overcometh, the same shall be clothed in white raiment; and I will not blot out his name out of the book of life, but I will confess his name before my Father, and before his angels."

In the glorious description of the holy city, the new Jerusalem which came down from God out of heaven, the gates of the city will not be shut at all by day for there shall be no night there. Into it will be brought the glory and honor of the nations, and those who enter and dwell in that city are spoken of as "they which are written in the Lamb's Book of Life." In this great passage from which we take our text, John speaks of the beast, the incarnation of iniquity and enmity to God, that came up out of the abyss with its death-stroke healed and that opened its mouth in blasphemy against God and made war with the saints. All the world worshipped it and said, "Who is like unto the beast?" But there were some who did not worship it, who penetrated its mask, discerned its guile and wickedness, and defied its power. These were the ones "whose names (are) written in the Book of Life of the Lamb slain from the foundation of the world."

Taken together, all these passages from the Book of Exodus to the Book of Revelation give us a picture of the people of God and the eternal security of the redeemed founded upon the love of God in Christ crucified for our sins, the Lamb slain from the foundation of the world.

II. To Have Our Name Written in the Lamb's Book of Life Is the Chief End of Life

On a late summer day in 1758, the Quaker George Fox met Oliver Cromwell riding through Hampton Park in London at the head of his guards. Fox said when he passed him, "I saw and felt a wave of death go forth against him."

A few days later the great Lord Protector lay dying at Whitehall Palace. His interest in the things of this world receded, and his soul fell back on itself as it advanced to the mysterious frontier of eternity. Nothing now to him that his voice had been the mightiest in Europe, making kings tremble. Nothing now to him the glory of Dunbar and Marsten Moor. The only thing that engaged his mind was the welfare of his immortal soul. On the second of September, he said to his chaplain, "Is it possible to fall from grace?" When the chaplain told him that it was not possible, he said, "I am safe, for I know that I was once in grace." The chief interest and concern of the great Lord Protector was to know that his name was written in the Lamb's Book of Life.

That is still a person's greatest concern, despite the fact that some people today think they have discovered that it is an unworthy concern. John Bunyan's Pilgrim who set out from the City of Destruction for the City of Life is now considered by some to have been a selfish and un-worthy man because he made the salvation of his own soul his chief end in life and set out by himself for the City of Life, leaving all others behind him. But John

Bunyan was eternally right. No person who has not himself or herself started for the City of Life will ever start others in that direction.

In his account of the last hours of the German patriot and statesman Karl Stein, who was outlawed by Napoleon with that celebrated phrase, "one named Stein," Andrew D. White said there was no mention of the salvation of the soul, for he took it for granted that his soul would be saved if it was worth saving. That comment is characteristic of the wisdom of this world that thinks it knows more than the Lord Jesus Christ himself. Every soul is, indeed, worth saving. The worth of every soul is measured by the blood of Christ shed on the cross to redeem it. But Christ is the only Savior of the soul. Every soul is worth saving, but no soul can save itself.

III. To Have Our Name Written in the Lamb's Book of Life Is the Highest of all Distinctions

The highest of all honors and distinctions is to have our name written in the Lamb's Book of Life. When those seventy disciples returned to Jesus and were rejoicing over the way in which they had been able to heal the sick and to cast out the evil spirits, Jesus told them to take no pride in that but to rejoice only that their names were written in heaven. That is the only honor, the only achievement, that abides. To multitudes who speak the English tongue, the most pleasing spot in Rome is the Protestant cemetery—that quiet, verdant, and shaded place of sepulchre just outside the walls, hard by the Pyramid of Caestius where Paul was beheaded. Down in one corner one comes upon the grave of the poet Shelly and not far from it the grave of the poet Keats. On his grave is that strange inscription, that epitaph which in his dying hour and in his disappointment Keats desired should be placed on his grave—"Here lies one whose name was writ in water." So far as poets go, that is not true, for the name of the man who wrote the "Ode on a Grecian Urn" will live as long as any of them. Yet in another sense that epitaph tells the story of all earthly renown and achievement. It is but a name writ in water. The wind blows, the ripple flows, and the name is gone. So it is that the highest fame, the only labor that endures, and the only cause for rejoicing is to have our names written in heaven—written in the Lamb's Book of Life never to be blotted out.

In that famous picture of what made Scotland great, "The Cotter's Saturday Night," Robert Burns shows us the family assembled around the family altar while the saintly father prays for his children. "Compared with this," he says, "how poor religion's pride."

> The Power incensed the pageant will desert,
> The pompous strain, the sacerdotal stole,
> But happily, in some cottage far apart,
> May hear well pleased the language of the soul;
> And in His Book of Life the inmates poor enroll.

What about that Book of Life? Have you made that your chief concern? Have you asked the Lamb of God to write your name in that book never to be blotted out? That is the will of God for us. "The world passeth away," John says, "and the lust thereof, but he that doeth the will of God abideth forever."

5

The Wrath of the Lamb

And [they] said to the mountains and rocks, 'Fall on us and hide us from the face of him that sitteth on the throne, and from the wrath of the Lamb. (Revelation 6:16)

Those of you who have visited the Sistine Chapel in the Vatican at Rome and have looked at the magnificent frescoes of Michelangelo—*the Creation of Man, Jonah, the Sibyls,* and the others—will be unlikely to forget his representation there of Christ as the austere Judge of the world, hurling the condemned and impenitent sinners into the place of punishment. We find it difficult to reconcile that Christ with the One who wept at the grave of Lazarus and took little children up in His arms and blessed them. So, when we come to this passage in the book of Revelation and read of men calling on the mountains and the rocks to fall on them and hide them from the wrath of the Lamb, we are at first troubled and shocked. These other presentations of the Lamb of God, the Lamb who opens the book of human destiny, the Lamb who is the bridegroom of the church, the Lamb who makes war on Satan, the Lamb who was slain for our salvation from the foundation of the world, the Lamb who is the light of heaven and whose song is its music— all these cause us little difficulty. But what about the wrath of the Lamb? The Lamb is the symbol of innocence, the most gentle and inoffensive of all creatures. How could a Lamb be angry? Yet the same book that tells us about the tenderness and the sacrificial love of the Lamb tells us also of the wrath of the Lamb.

At first, I thought I might leave out this representation from this series on the Lamb of God. It would be easy to do that and, no doubt, very acceptable to the majority of my hearers. But the interrogation of a good conscience is something that no person—and especially no preacher— can ever ignore. Conscience could not approve if we turned away from this presentation of Christ. It represents tremendous and important truths of the Gospel–the truth that we must all stand before the judgment seat of Christ; the truth that it is a dreadful thing to fall into the hands of the living God; the truth that those who finally reject the love of God in Christ must experience His righteous and eternal judgment.

When the sixth seal was opened on the seven-sealed book of history and destiny, there were convulsions upon the earth. There was a great earthquake; the sun became black as sackcloth; the moon became as blood; the stars of heaven fell unto the earth; the heavens departed as a scroll when it is rolled together; and every mountain and island were moved out of their places. These are the prelude to the final judgment of God and the great day of His wrath. In that day the small and the great, the kings of the earth, great people, rich people, the captains, the mighty, the slaves, and the free will hide in the dens and in the rocks of the mountains and will cry to the mountains and rocks, "Fall on us, and hide us from the face of him that sitteth on the throne, and from the wrath of the Lamb; for the great day of his wrath is come; and who shall be able to stand?" The wrath of the Lamb, then, presents to us the great truth of God's future and final judgment upon evil and upon evil men and women.

I. A Law of God's Universe

This is not a doctrine upon which we stumble suddenly in the Bible, out of keeping with all thought and experience, but one that belongs to the thought and instinct of the human race everywhere. If an effort were made to unite in one all the creeds and religions and philosophies of the past and the present, the future judgment would be the doctrine upon which the greatest number would agree. It is a truth revealed in the Scriptures, and of all the truths in the Scriptures—no matter how we may take offense at it and in practice deny it—it is the one above all others that we conceive of with the least difficulty.

In the famous sermon which made the Roman Governor Felix tremble, Paul preached to him of "righteousness, temperance, and judgment to come." If Felix trembled, it was because of that last division of Paul's sermon. He struck that great chord which God has strung in every heart, the conviction that there is a future judgment. When the pronouncement of judgment is made by the Word of

God, the human heart and conscience answer it. "Deep
calleth unto deep." Christian doctrine plumbed to the
depths when it laid the foundation of future punishment.
As someone aptly put it, "Justice is like the Kingdom of
God. It is not without us as a fact; it is within us as a great
yearning!"

One might say that there are four great moral and religious convictions: there is a God; human beings are
immortal souls; there is a hereafter; and the soul will be
judged. There are judgments, very serious and solemn
judgments, even in this world. The way of the transgressor is hard here, as well as hereafter. But the judgments of
this world are not the final judgment. The apostle Paul
said, "Some men's sins are manifest, going before them to
judgment, and some they follow after." That is, sometimes even in this world we can see the transgressor
punished. But not always. The final punishment and judgment must take place in the world to come. That is what
the Bible means by the frequent phrase, "the wrath to
come." Not that God is angry or passionate like us, but
His face is set against the doers of iniquity, and the Judge
of the earth must do right.

As you go into the harbor of Cobb, Ireland, you can see
on the top of a hill a white shaft which marks the grave of
Charles Wolfe, the author of those almost perfect lines
on "The Burial of Sir John Moore at Corunna." Wolfe
was a preacher of great ability, as well as a poet. In a
sermon on the last judgment, based on the text from
Ecclesiastes, "Because sentence against an evil work is not
executed speedily, therefore, the heart of the sons of men
is fully set in them to do evil," Wolfe in this striking way
said, "The judgments of God fall often enough in this
world to let us know that God judges, but seldom often

enough to let us know that there must be a judgment hereafter."

There are four reasons why justice here is not final. One is that some of the worst sins are not against the natural order but against the spiritual order. Against these sins time and human laws take no account. Again, the courts of justice in this world are not infallible. On occasion they have made tragic mistakes in their findings and in their judgments. This also is true, that the sentences pronounced here are merely gestures in the direction of justice. What legislature, what court, knows what, (exactly), is the just penalty that ought to be imposed for a particular transgression? Here, too, the guilty often escape. On the domes of many of the county courthouses of our land, you can see the statue of Justice, blindfolded, with the balances in her hand. That is the symbol of our effort to do justice and a symbol, too, of our reverence for justice. But no one imagines that everything that transpires under the domes of those courthouses is in keeping with the symbol of justice on their roofs. No, it will take the judgment that follows after, the final judgment of the world to come, to do perfect justice and to inflict the penalty that is deserved.

II. AN INFERENCE OF THE GOSPEL

The implications and inferences of the gospel of redemption are all on the side of a final judgment on sin. If we are offered salvation in Christ, then there must be the opposite condition. Otherwise, there would be no sense in the offer of salvation.

If God gave His only begotten Son that we might not perish but have everlasting life, then a fate must be possible for us that is the opposite of everlasting life. If Christ came to save us, then there must be a condition of woe and unhappiness from which we are saved. The supreme fact in our Christian faith is the Cross. But who can behold the Lamb of God in His agony in Gethsemane, or deserted and forsaken on the cross, knowing that His suffering and death were the price He paid to redeem us from sin, and not recognize that if such a great price as this was necessary, then how great is our need and how dark is the fate from which He came to redeem us? If there is no calamity that threatens the human soul, then Calvary was too great a remedy, too tragic a price for Christ to pay. Then it was out of all proportion to our condition and need.

III. THE TEACHING OF JESUS

When you are troubled about this part of the Christian revelation, it is well to turn back to the teachings of Jesus himself. Future judgment, future punishment is, as we have seen, an inevitable inference and assumption of the great Christian doctrines. It is also explicitly taught in the Bible and by Christ himself above all others. He is the chief teacher. The same Jesus who took little children up in His arms and blessed them, who said, "Come unto me, and I will give you rest," and who pronounced the Beatitudes, spoke the strongest words concerning future judgment and future punishment.

Jesus said much about duty in this life, but always in connection with destiny. Of His thirty parables, twelve leave people not only condemned and punished here, but sentenced for the life to come. Christ said of Judas that his sin was so great it would have been better for him not to have been born. He said of others that their sin was so great it would have been better for them that a millstone had been hung about their neck and they had been drowned in the depths of the sea, rather than face the judgment of God and the wrath of the Lamb. In His two great pronouncements on the subject of the judgment to come—the parable of Dives and Lazarus and the appearance of all people before Him on the Day of Judgment—Jesus taught that there is an unbridgeable gulf in the life to come between two kinds of people: those who are accepted by God and those who are rejected by Him. The same Jesus who says, "Come, ye blessed of my Father," also says, "Depart from me; I never knew you."

There is no possible way in which you can discount or minimize these teachings of Jesus. To say that He just adapted Himself to popular ideas then current on this subject but did not hold them Himself, is to make Him a false teacher and an impostor. To say that He really believed in future punishment but was mistaken, leaves Him an ignorant man. Either Jesus is an infallible teacher, and there is a future judgment and punishment, or there is no future punishment, and Jesus is a fallible, mistaken teacher, and the Bible is an untrustworthy book.

This final revelation of the righteousness of God, the full manifestation of the law of Justice, is inevitable in the case of those who have rejected Christ as Savior, who have scorned His love and His atonement. These are the ones who call upon the mountains and the rocks to fall upon them and to hide them from the face of Him that sits upon the throne and from the wrath of the Lamb. Mountains and rocks here may be figurative language. But how tremendous these figures of speech are! Think of people calling upon the mountains and the rocks to crush them and annihilate them, rather than that they should have to stand in the presence of the offended and rejected Lamb of God! For you and me this has a timeless, practical meaning, for we shall all stand before the judgment seat of Christ.

In the Gospels, Christ does not generally seem to have been shocked and amazed at sin, as we might suppose He would have been. He often met with great sinners and spoke calmly of sin. Rarely do we find in Him a trace of surprise or astonishment or anger. But there was one exception. It was when He spoke of that sin which to us at times may appear to be the least of all sins, but which He regarded as the most fearful sin of all, the sin of unbelief, of rejecting Him. That people should see and know their guilt, know they must die and pass to judgment, and yet do nothing—that they should refuse Him as their Saviour and trample the blood of His Atonement under foot— that was what amazed Him. For all sins and all sinners, the deepest and the foulest, the blood of Christ avails. He is able to save completely and forever all those who come to Him. But when people scorn this remedy, then there is nothing left but a "certain fearful looking for of judgment"—the wrath of the Lamb.

In your own recollection you may have felt that the most moving, solemn manifestation of wrath and anger was that of the godly father or mother who loved you and toiled for you and prayed over you and wept over you, but whose soul was stirred to the depths by righteous indignation at some misdeed you had done. What, then, can compare with the displeasure of an offended Savior? What will it be to face a rejected Lord and Savior? What will it be to look upon Him whom you have pierced and despised?

In Cardinal Newman's great study of the last judgment, "The Dream of Gerontius," the soul that is being conducted by the angels to the judgment seat, wonders why he has no feeling of fear; whereas, in life, the judgment was ever before him, and the Judge seemed severe to him even in the crucifix. The angel tells him it is because he feared and thought of the judgment in this earthly life that the judgment has no fear for him now. The perfect love of Christ which he had accepted has cast out all fear.

How, then, will you look upon the Lamb of God on that great day? Will you call upon the rocks to fall on you and hide you from His righteous judgment? Or will you call upon Him as your rock and refuge of salvation?

> Rock of Ages, cleft for me,
> Let me hide myself in thee.

In the other great pictures of the last judgment in this book of Revelation, John saw the dead, the small and the great, stand before the throne, and the books were opened. That is the great certainty. We shall all stand before the judgment seat of Christ. Where you will stand a year from today no one knows. You cannot be certain that you will be here next Sunday. You cannot be certain that you will be here when the benediction is pronounced today. But there is one thing of which we can all be certain, and that is, we shall all appear before Christ at the last judgment. In this great picture of that judgment, John said, "The books were opened, . . . and the dead were judged out of those things which were written in the books, according to their works." "And another book was opened, which is the book of life." This Book of Life records the names of the redeemed, all those who have believed in Jesus as the Lamb of God, have followed Him upon earth, and now are worthy to walk with Him in white. In that judgment they have no fear, for they know His redeeming love. They said a long time ago, and now more than ever realize the meaning of it, "I know whom I have believed, and am persuaded that he is able to keep that which I have committed unto him against that day."

6

The Lamb and His Bride

Come hither, I will show thee the bride,
the Lamb's wife. (Revelation 21:9)

The world began and the world will end with a marriage. Until that final marriage of the Lamb and His bride, marriage never wears out, for it strikes the universal chord of love. We think of the brides of the Bible—of Eve, the mother of all living; of beautiful Rebekah and lovely Rachel; and the bride in the Song of Solomon. Whenever people hear the music of the *Wedding March* they turn to look. Let it be known that a marriage is being celebrated in this church, and at once a crowd will gather on the sidewalk across the street to see the bride and the bridegroom come out. It is a long time since Adam awoke out of a deep sleep and found

his bride by his hitherto solitary side. Marriage never
wears out.

This week the interest of the whole world, especially
the millions in the British Empire and all those who speak
the English tongue, will travel to Westminster Abbey in
London, where the blue-eyed Princess Elizabeth will marry
her chosen consort, Philip Mountbatten.* What a place
for a wedding! We know it as Westminster Abbey, but its
ecclesiastical name is the Abbey of St. Peter, going clear
back to the seventh century. Thus, the most famous church
of Protestantism bears the same name as the most famous
church of Roman Catholicism. The present structure goes
back to the year 1045 when the church was commenced
by Edward the Confessor. Passing through the venerable
cloisters, you enter the nave of the Abbey. At once you
seem to lose yourself in the shadows of antiquity. All English history is, as it were, embodied here in stone. All
around you are effigies of monks, knights, and Crusaders;
the busts and graves of poets, statesmen, philosophers,
soldiers; and here are the tombs of the kings and queens.
Once their scepters ruled millions. Now they are voice-
less and crumbled into dust. Here the kings were crowned
amid great splendor as they sat upon the Stone of Scone,
and here with pomp and ceremony at which the great
conqueror Death must have laughed, they were gathered
to their fathers. Here princes were baptized, and here the
kings and the queens were married. Next Thursday in
this treasury of mortality and humility—a place that pro-
claims the emptiness of mortal renown and the certainty
of oblivion, that reminds us that the paths of glory lead
but to the grave—the princess will be married. Two thou-

---

* This sermon was preached in 1947.

sand guests gathered in the Abbey and millions all over
the world listening to the music and the vows will bestow
their prayers and good wishes upon the young woman
who one day will wear the crown of Mary and Elizabeth
and Charlotte and Anne and Victoria.

Tonight we think of another marriage, the last of all
marriages, consummated with all heaven and earth as spec-
tators. Only two thousand have been invited to the
marriage next Thursday at Westminster Abbey, but all
people are invited to the marriage of the Lamb and His
bride. The last things have come to pass. The enemies of
God have been judged and cast into their place of doom.
The souls of the martyrs, beheaded for the witness of
Jesus, have come forth to live and to reign with Christ.
Before the great white throne, the small and the great,
the living and the dead have been judged. The new heaven
and new earth have come down from God out of heaven,
prepared as a bride adorned for her husband. All sorrow
and sin and the curse have passed away, and the tabernacle of God is with men. Then comes the invitation
from one of the seven angels, "Come hither, I will show
thee the bride, the Lamb's wife."

These words mark the conclusion of the eternal court-
ship between Christ and His church. Christ chose the
church from before the foundation of the world, redeemed
her from her sin and the fall by His death, washed her
white with His precious blood, and now presents her unto
Himself without spot or wrinkle, His blood-bought, glorious bride. The sorrow and travail of the church are
ended, and the long night of weeping has become the
morn of song.

This symbolic marriage and its feast mark the goal of
redemption. All the divine revelation and ordinances, the

tabernacle and temple rites, the prophecies, the incarnation of Jesus, the miracles, the Atonement, the Resurrection, the gift of the Holy Spirit—all were granted and decreed and enacted for this great end. All looked forward to this glorious day when the triumphant Lamb of God takes His bride, the church.

The thought of the church as the bride of Christ is a beautiful and favorite figure of speech in the Bible. In the prophecy of Isaiah God says, "O Israel, fear not, for I have redeemed thee; I have called thee by name; thou art mine." This closest and most tender of human relationships is used to express the relationship between Christ and His church. The apostle Paul tells husbands that they are the head of the wife, as Christ is the Head of the church, which is His mystical body. He entreats them to love their wives "even as Christ also loved the church and gave himself for it, that he might sanctify and cleanse it" and "might present it to himself a glorious church, not having spot, or wrinkle, or any such thing, but that it should be holy and without blemish."

These expressions bring before us the lofty scriptural conception of the church and its relationship to Christ. The church is far more than a building, a denomination, or a congregation. It is more than the whole visible organized church on the face of the whole earth. It is the precious blood-bought and finally triumphant bride of Christ.

There are two conceptions of the church. One is that of the visible church, made up of all who profess the true religion together with their children. That church and its members we know and see. There is also the invisible church, made up of all redeemed souls that have been, are, or will yet be gathered into one under Christ, the

Head of which it is the body, the fullness of Him who fills
all things. Although Protestantism historically and theo-
logically has had very high views of the church, those
views are being lost sight of today. The church faces the
risk of its complete secularization, which would make it
just an assembly, an agency of reform, an instrument of
education and culture. Hence, we must get back to the
New Testament concept of the church as the bride of
Christ.

Christ died for you and me as individuals, and no one is
a Christian until that person can say, "He loved me and
gave himself for me." But Christ died also for a company
of people, for the flock of God, for the church of God.
He died to secure for Himself a redeemed and sanctified
nation that will reign with Him forever. This glorious
consummation presents to us not merely a great end, but
an ideal of life for the present and visible church.

I. THE PURITY OF THE CHURCH

First of all, the figure of the bride speaks of the purity
of the church. Brides are always clad in white, signifying
purity and righteousness. The church is an exotic plant in
a wicked world and must have deep rootage and be well-
watered if it is to flourish. Always in the history of the
Jewish nation there was a drift toward the world, toward
idolatry, against which the law and the prophets warned
and thundered. If the church is to keep her garments
clean, she must resist that world-drift and obey the command of the Scriptures, "Come out from among them,
and be ye separate."

Protestantism began with a great protest against a corrupt and impure church. Today its peril is that it should

cease to protest against anything and should accommodate itself to the life of the world. The church has always done most for the world when it had the least to do with the world. Its moral and spiritual authority and influence are in proportion, not to its organization, its buildings, its rituals, its numbers, its fashion, and wealth, but to its separation from the world.

II. THE FIDELITY OF THE CHURCH TO HER BRIDEGROOM

Again, the church, as the bride of Christ, must be faithful to her Lord and Bridegroom. She must be faithful to those great truths which Christ has committed to her. St. Paul spoke of the "glorious gospel of the blessed God, which was committed to my trust." The church is the custodian of the great truths of redemption. In all the ages she has found it necessary to have creeds and confessions as "a declaration of truth, a protest against error, a bond of union and means of growth, and to hand down uncorrupted and undiminished the truth once for all delivered unto the saints."

Yet today we are constantly being told that creeds and confessions of faith are no longer necessary, that they are a hindrance rather than a help to the church. If this is so, it must be for one of two reasons: either it is impossible to state and declare the truth of the gospel and show its difference from all other religious systems; or, there is no longer any necessity for such a statement, and the church is no longer assailed by subtle and dangerous foes that press upon her from the outside and assail her from within her own walls. But we know all too well that these foes are still here. The church could not have survived in the past without a definite witness to Christ and the truth, and it cannot exist and do its work today without such a witness. To ask the church now to give up the formal statements of her belief would be like telling a regiment to strike its flag in the face of the foe.

III. THE CHURCH AND ITS AGE-LONG WAIT FOR THE COMING OF THE BRIDEGROOM

The church must be faithful in the age-long wait for the return of her Lord and the coming of her Bridegroom. That was the charge Christ gave to the disciples and to the church. "Occupy till I come." Preaching in St. Paul's Cathedral on the subject of Christ's return, Canon Liddon once said, "Let us turn the key in the west door of the cathedral, if Christ is not coming back in glory."

In one of the greatest of all stories, Homer's *Odyssey*, the King of Ithaca, Odysseus, shrewd in counsel and a mighty fighter in the Trojan War, starts to go back to his home and his bride on pent-up Ithaca. But storms and unfavorable winds drive him off his course, until, losing all his ships and men, he arrives on the island of Calypso. After eight years there, he is permitted to depart. At length, after divers adventures, he arrives home at Ithaca to find his wife, Penelope, who has been tempted and beset by numerous suitors, still faithful to him.

The church in the world is beset by numerous suitors who would seek to win her from her Lord and Bridegroom, both in the doctrines that she teaches and in the life that she leads. Her work, therefore, is to be faithful, to do the work of Christ, to occupy till He comes. Whether He comes in the second, the third, or the fourth watch— the watch just before the dawning, the hardest watch of all, when men's hearts are perplexed and even the elect are deceived—blessed is that servant, and blessed is that church, whom when He comes, He will find waiting and watching.

IV. THE JOY AND LOVE OF THE MARRIAGE

A wedding is an occasion of joy and love. A wedding without love or joy on the part of the bride and the bridegroom would be a sad and distressing thing. It would be no true marriage at all.

> The Bride eyes not her garment,
> But her dear bridegroom's face.

A great need of the church today is a revival of love for the person of Christ, her Lord and Bridegroom. Not merely love for the glory of His person, or excellence of His doctrine, or the sway of His influence in human history, but for Christ as her Redeemer. The only reason for our love is that He loved us and gave Himself for us.

Love for Christ springs out of our knowledge of Christ as our Redeemer. Jesus once let a woman who was a sinner touch Him, washing His feet with her tears and wiping them with the hairs of her head, kissing them and anointing them with ointment. When Simon the Pharisee rebuked Him for this, Jesus told the story of a creditor who had two debtors, one of whom owed him five hundred pence and the other fifty. When they had nothing to pay, he forgave them both. "Tell me therefore," Jesus said to Simon, "which of them will love him most?" Simon, somewhat reluctantly, answered, "I suppose that he, to whom he forgave most." Jesus told him that he had judged rightly and said, "Her sins, which are many, are forgiven;

for she loved much; but to whom little is forgiven, the same loveth little."

This is the source and fountain of our love for Christ— a consciousness of what He has done for us as sinners on the cross. Some churches are as different from one another as noonday is from midnight, and mid-summer from austere winter. The reason is that in one church, the atmosphere is created by love for Christ as the Redeemer, while in another church that atmosphere is wanting. You need not listen long to any preacher or worship long in any congregation to find out whether or not redeeming love is the great theme, and "shall be to the end."

At the wedding in Cana of Galilee that Jesus blessed and where He performed His first miracle by turning the water into wine, the ruler of the feast called the bridegroom and said to him, "Thou hast kept the good wine until now." The best wine for the soul and for the church is always in the future. Clouds and darkness hang over the world today. Wars and rumors of wars abound and people's hearts are failing them. But for the church, the horizon is always bright with the promise of the coming glory. The Bridegroom says to His bride, "Lift up your head, for your redemption draweth nigh." "Awake, awake; put on thy strength, O Zion; put on thy beautiful garments, O Jerusalem, the holy city."

The bride that John saw when he was invited to that final marriage was the church, the city of God. "I saw a new heaven and a new earth, for the first heaven and the first earth were passed away, and there was no more sea. And I, John, saw the holy city, the new Jerusalem, coming down from God out of heaven, prepared as a bride adorned for her husband." Then the whole earth will no longer be called "Forsaken" or "Desolate," but "Beulah," that is, "married," for the Lord will be light in it and the earth will be married to Christ. Then God shall wipe away all tears from every eye. Then nations shall learn war no more. They shall turn their swords into plowshares and their spears into pruning hooks. "They shall not hurt nor destroy in all my holy mountain, for the earth shall be full of the knowledge of the Lord, as the waters cover the sea."

Let us, therefore, be faithful members of the church of Christ. Let us march and sing as people who are above the din and wail of this present world and who have caught the note of that far-off distant song that John heard in heaven when the Lamb took His bride, "Alleluia! for the Lord God omnipotent reigneth! Let us be glad and rejoice, and give honor to him; for the marriage of the Lamb is come, and his wife hath made herself ready. . . . Blessed are they which are called unto the marriage supper of the Lamb."

You all have an invitation from God the Father to be present at the marriage supper of the Lamb. Will you be there? Or, like those persons of whom Jesus spoke in His parable of the Great Supper, whom when they were invited to the king's supper, "made light of it," will you, too, make light of it? Will you not answer the King's invitation, and go in to the banqueting house and hail the Lamb slain from the foundation of the world and His blood-bought, glorious, and now triumphant bride?

7

The Light of the Lamb

And the Lamb is the light thereof.   (Revelation 21:23)

The conclusion of the Book of Revelation is like a beautiful sunset at the close of a stormy day. The trumpets of doom sound no more. All the seven golden vials of God's wrath and judgment have been poured out. No more are there fearful signs in the heavens and tribulations and calamities upon earth. Hostile armies clash no more in battle, for war on earth and war in heaven is forever over. The kingdom of evil and darkness with all its agents and representatives, the devil, the dragon, the beast, the wicked and the impenitent of the earth, have gone down to rise no more. The first heaven and the first earth and all that they imply—their whole order—have passed away. In their places has come the new order, the eternal order, the new heaven and the new earth, the holy city of God coming down from God out of heaven, like a bride adorned for her husband.

What a city it is which is described here in this great vision! Ephesus on the Cayster, where John perhaps wrote the Apocalypse which had been granted him on the Island of Patmos, was a noble city with its famous white marble Corso, over which you can still walk today, and its wonderful Temple of Diana, gleaming afar with its soft radiance of a star. Antioch the Golden, on the fast-flowing Orontes, where the disciples were first called Christians, was a glorious city; so was Alexandria in Egypt; and Jerusalem with its temple; and Athens with its Parthenon; and Rome on its seven hills. But what are they compared with this city?

Here is a city which stretched for fifteen hundred miles in every direction, and whose length and breadth and height were equal. It stood upon twelve foundations, garnished with all manner of precious stones, with the names of the twelve apostles of the Lamb inscribed upon them. The gates of the city, which were never closed, three on the north, three on the south, three on the east, and three on the west, were each a flaming pearl and inscribed upon them were the names of the twelve tribes of Israel, for this city summed up and represented the whole glory of redemption.

In ancient as in modern cities today, there was a sad contrast between the splendor and magnificence of the city and the wretchedness of the inhabitants. Whether you look on Babylon in its might, Jerusalem in its sacred beauty, or Rome in its glory, you are looking upon a city all of whose inhabitants will pass away like the leaves of autumn long before the city itself disappears. For upon them all is the sentence of death, and in them all are the ravages of sin. But here no such contrast exists. The inhabitants are as great and glorious as the city they inhabit.

John tells us much about this great city, but I think the most remarkable thing is what he tells us about the lighting of the city. The midday sun did not illuminate its streets, nor did the orient moon or the glorious company of the stars discover its towers and palaces. "The city had no need of the sun, neither of the moon, to shine in it, for the glory of God did lighten it, and the Lamb is the light thereof. And the nations of them which are saved shall walk in the light of it, and the kings of the earth do bring their glory and honor into it. And the gates of it shall not be shut at all by day, for there shall be no night there." Where the Lamb is, there is no night.

Thus the glory of the redeemed society is the glory of the Lamb of God, that is, Christ crucified. The Scriptures always leave Christ in the highest place. Before the foundations of the world He was forever in the glory of the Father. When He came into the world to redeem it, the angels worshipped Him. "He is the First and the Last, the Beginning and the End, the Alpha and the Omega, the Lord of life and death and hell. Since that is always the place that the Scriptures give to Christ—always the pre-eminence—it is not strange that here in the city of God, the goal of the ages and of redemption, Christ is the light.

I. The Lamb Is the Light of the Perfect Society and the Final Order

Our human race, conscious of the imperfection of the present order, has ever been haunted by the thought of the perfect order that some day will arise to supersede the present one. We cannot contemplate the present order as an eternal order, for that would seem to advertise the failure of God and the triumph of sin. It would mean the perpetual recurrence of what now is. How many dreams there have been of that perfect order—the New Atlantis of Bacon, the Republic of Plato, the Utopia of Moore. These are some of the dreams that men have dreamed. In spite of hope deferred, in spite of the long procession of wars and cruelties and oppressions and abominations, mankind has refused to be stripped of its expectations of the future. The tears through which its eyes have beheld afar off the city of God, the reign of justice and love, have only served to gild its towers and turrets with a more resplendent glory.

There is something here
   Unfathomed by the cynic's sneer,
Something that gives our feeble light
   A high immunity from night;
Something that leaps life's narrow bars
   To claim its birthright with the hosts of heaven;
A seed of sunshine that can leaven
   Our earthly dullness with the beams of stars,
And glorify our clay
   With light from fountains older than the day.
A conscience more divine than we,
   A gladness fed with secret tears,
A vexing forward reaching sense
   Of some more noble performance;
A light across the sea,
   Which haunts the soul and will not let it be,
Still beaconing from the heights of undegenerate years.

But there is a great contrast between the city of human hope and expectation and the city of God and between humanity's ideal commonwealth and that of the Apocalypse. Our perfect order is to rise, so we are told, out of the present order. It will be the result of ages of struggle and strife and suffering and development, the goal we reach after the long journey. But the city of God is not a perfect, human city, but a redeemed and regenerated city. Here is not mere protection and immunity from evil things, but a redeemed race, a new creation. The new order is not to rise out of the present order, but is to supersede it altogether. Listen to the music of that heavenly world! Of what do its inhabitants sing? What powers do they claim as the secret of their bliss and freedom? Here below we hear much of the power of science, of education, of good environment, of good government, of good example, of internationalism. All that is good. But in the song that goes up from those multitudes gathered out of every tribe and people and kindred and tongue, the ten thousand times ten thousand, I catch no echo of such things as these. None of these things is acclaimed in that song. None of them is praised. Of what do these multitudes sing? What powers do they acclaim as the secret of their strength and splendor? The only song I hear is this: "Worthy is the Lamb that was slain to receive power, and riches and wisdom and strength and honor and glory and blessing." Only one throne is worshipped, the throne of the Lamb. Only one name is named, the name that is above every name. Only one song echoes there, the song of Moses and the Lamb. Only one glory shines there, and that is the light of the Lamb:

> Where the Lamb on high is seated,
>   By ten thousand voices greeted,
> Lord of Lord and King of Kings:
>   Son of Man they crown, they crown him;

Son of God they own, they own him;
With his name the palace rings.

II. THE LAMB IS THE LIGHT OF THE LIFE WE SHALL LEAD IN HEAVEN

We have seen how the Lamb is the light and the strength of the redeemed society. But now, in a more personal sense, the Lamb is also the light of the life we shall lead there.

It is frequently said that there is a marked subsidence today in the tide of interest in the life to come and an increasing agnosticism, or even disbelief, concerning it. If so, it is certainly not because of any change in the order of human life. It is still "appointed unto all men once to die," and if that "once to die" means once for all, or once and forever, then, indeed, every trumpet of hope and expectation must be muted. If there is a fading interest in the life to come, it is accompanied by a fading interest in Christ as the Redeemer. If Christ is only our inspirer, our teacher, or our example, then the goal of existence is the knowledge of truth. But if Christ is our Redeemer, then the goal is Christ himself. The end of the Christian life is to be with Him and see Him as He is. If you cut out of the Apostles' Creed, "And in the life everlasting," you extinguish the light of every other affirmation and declaration of that great summary of Christian belief.

The great believers always liked to emphasize the truth that the goal and consummation of the Christian life is to be with Christ and to behold His face. So St. Paul declared that for him to die would be great gain, because it meant to depart and be with Christ. So St. Peter expressed the hope that readers might be found "unto praise and honor and glory at the appearing of Jesus Christ, whom having not seen, ye love." And so St. John wrote, "Beloved, now are we the sons of God, and it doth not yet appear what we shall be, but we know that when he shall appear we shall be like him for we shall see him as he is." The way, then, to revive faith in immortality is to revive faith in Christ as the Redeemer.

A faith that is centered upon Christ as the Redeemer will always be interested in the contemplation of the life to come. When Marco Polo, the famous Venetian traveler and explorer of the thirteenth century, lay on his death bed, he was urged by his attendants and confessors to recant and withdraw the stories he had told about the wonders of China and the other lands of Asia. But he refused to do so, and said, "I have not told half of what I saw." Whatever heaven is like and wherever it is, this much is certain: we shall never be able to tell half—no, not even a hundredth part—of it.

One meaning of light is knowledge. If the Lamb is our light in heaven, then how great will be our knowledge. A little child in heaven with the Lamb of God for only five minutes will know far more than Moses, Isaiah, Paul, Augustine, and Calvin together knew in this life, for all truth will shine reflected in the face of Christ. Here we see as in a glass darkly, just a dim reflection, only fitful gleams of the truth, but there we shall see "face to face," that is, we shall behold Him who is the Light of the world and the Light of heaven.

In His light we shall see the meaning of His cross. As redeemed people we know now that the Cross is the greatest accomplishment of God and of Christ. We lay hold of it by faith, but then all the depth and riches of the wisdom and the power of God in the redemption of sinners,

now unsearchable to you and me, will be made manifest.
Then, and not till then, we shall know how great was our
need, how deep our sin, and how much we owe to Christ.
If we can judge from the few glimpses of heaven afforded
us in the Bible, from the far-off strains of the heavenly
songs that float down to us, then that is going to be the
greatest experience of heaven—to realize just what it was
for Christ to seek and to save the lost. To that one theme
all the anthems of heaven are set.

In the light of the Lamb, we are going to understand
many things that are hid from us now. "In that day,"
Christ said, "ye shall ask me nothing." Here, how many
questions must wait for an answer! How many problems
can never be solved here! How many providences can
never be understood here! But then, when we look into
the face of the Lamb and know as we are known, we shall
at last understand. The light of the Lamb will lift all
shadows from our faces, all questions from our minds.
Then we shall venerate the wisdom and adore the goodness of the decrees of God both for our life and for the
life of the world.

> I'll bless the hand that guided,
>   I'll bless the heart that planned,
> When throned where glory dwelleth
>   In Immanuel's land.

III. The Light of the Lamb Can Be Our Light Even Now

The light of the Lamb can be our light even now. Not
in the sense of the final glorious revelation, about which
we have been speaking, of the love and power of God, but

the light by which we can live now, the light of our present life. Eternal life can begin now. You know what Paul said, speaking of the heavenly life, "We shall . . . bear the image of the heavenly." Another translation of that is, "Let us . . . bear the image of the heavenly," and that means now.

The supreme disclosure of God's love and power is the sacrificial love exemplified by Christ on the cross. Jesus said, "He that followeth me shall not walk in darkness." If we follow him, we shall live, even now, in the light of the Lamb. What we mean is that the law of Christ will be our guide and standard of life.

On the banks of the Seine in the very heart of Paris beneath a gilded dome rest the ashes of the restless Napoleon. Old banners, yellow with age, grimy with the smoke of battle, and rent by shot and shell, stand like sentinels about the tomb of him whose conquests they commemorate. In the marble walls that surround the sarcophagus are cut the names of his battles and victories—Marengo, Lodi, Jena, Austerlitz, and the Pyramids. People of all nations come and look with awe upon the coffin of red stone that contains the mortal relics of him whose armies overran the world. Through heavy windows of yellow glass, the golden sunlight streams down upon the silent chamber, as if to reflect the effulgence of immortal fame.

But there is a light that never shines there, a light that never shone in the face of him whose dust reposes there. We think of his empress, sacrificed to his ambition. We think of him standing on his lone rock in the wastes of the South Atlantic, wondering if anyone in the world really loved him. We think of the trails of blood and death that marked his advance and retreat from the Pyrenees to Moscow, from Germany to Italy, from the Pyramids to

Mt. Tabor. We behold the light of power, the light of military genius, the light of adulation, the light of earthly fame, but not a ray of that light that when all other lights have gone out, abides to cheer and to bless. No light of the Lamb, no light of sacrificial love, shines over that marble tomb. But today I could take you and you could take me, to some quiet acre of God where, beneath a modest stone with no wondering throngs pressing about to gaze upon it, sleeps the dust of those whose influence is unending, whose companionship abides forever, and whose light never goes out because theirs was a life that followed in the footsteps of the Lamb.

Yes, that is the way to live. This world is a dark place, but you can light it up as multitudes before you have done: by faith in Christ the Lamb of God as your Savior and Redeemer; by obedience to His will; and by following Him from day to day. This is the path of the just and the path of the justified "that shineth more and more unto the perfect day."

8

The Song of the Lamb

They sing the song of Moses the servant of God,
and the song of the Lamb. (Revelation 15:3)

Walking sometime ago through one of the old cemeteries at Georgetown, near Washington, I came upon a grave with an inscription that ended with these words from the book of Revelation: "They sing a new song." Fitting and happy words for an inscription on the grave of a true Christian! That was the song that John heard those who won the victory over the beast, singing as they stood upon the sea of glass mingled with fire before the throne of God. "They [sang] the song of Moses the servant of God, and the song of the Lamb."

The Bible is full of songs. Christianity does not invite you to a funeral or to stand against a wailing wall. It invites you to a jubilation, to a celebration of the triumph of righteousness. The Bible echoes with glorious song. At the creation, the morning stars sang together, and all the

sons of God sang for joy. Moses sang his great song cel-
ebrating the deliverance of Israel out of the Red Sea and
the overthrow of Pharaoh and his chariots. Deborah sang
her song of triumph over the defeat of Sisera and his
hosts. Hannah sang over the birth of Samuel. The great
Messianic predictions of the prophets are magnificent
songs. Before Christ was born, Mary sang and Zacharias
sang. At His birth, the multitude of the angels sang over
the fields near Bethlehem. Jesus and His disciples sang a
hymn in the Upper Room before they went out to
Gethsemane. Paul and Silas sang praises to God at midnight in the dungeon at Philippi, their backs raw and
bleeding from the cruel scourging they had received, and
"all the prisoners heard them singing." Today we come to
the grand climax of all those biblical songs, the song of
Moses and the Lamb, the song which celebrates the down-
fall of the kingdom of evil and the triumph of the kingdom
of Christ.

Of all the passages of the Bible, this is one of the most
sublime and most beautiful. John saw what looked like a
sea of glass mingled with fire, and those that had gotten
the victory over the beast, over his image, and over his
mark, standing on the sea of glass and having the harps of
God. And they sang the song of Moses and the song of
the Lamb, saying, "Great and marvelous are thy works,
Lord God Almighty; just and true are thy ways, thou
King of saints. Who shall not fear thee, O Lord, and
glorify thy name? For thou only art holy; for all nations
shall come and worship before thee; for thy judgments
are made manifest."

At the end of this great song, the temple of God in
heaven opened and seven white-robed angels appeared
with golden vials of the wrath of God. The angels went

forth to pour their vials of judgment upon the earth. Then followed signs and wonders, plagues and wars, and eruptions of Satanic powers. But at the end this rebellion and unrighteousness were overthrown. Then John heard the voice of a vast multitude singing a great Song, "Alleluia! The Lord God Omnipotent, reigneth!" "The kingdoms of this world are become the kingdoms of our Lord and His Christ, and he shall reign forever and forever."

There is no reason to think that by the song of Moses is meant the song that Moses sang over the drowning of Pharaoh and his hosts in the Red Sea. Nor is the song of Moses and the Lamb a song that the Lamb sings. It is rather a song of wonder and rejoicing by all the redeemed over the consummation of God's great plan for the overthrow of the kingdom of evil and the salvation of mankind. Its great theme is what Moses and the Old Testament stood for in the preparation for that plan, what Christ did upon the cross and what He will yet do in bringing that plan to completion. Listening to the grand harmonies of this song, we discern three dominant notes: the holiness of God, the redemption of God, and the ways of God

I. THE HOLINESS OF GOD

This great choir sang, "Who shall not fear thee, O Lord, and glorify thy name? For thou only art holy." To you and me holiness is a cold, perhaps even unpleasant, word. We have a certain native resentment for lives better than our own, for they seem to rebuke us. One who is holy and blameless seems to be, and is, remote from our own life. Yet God, who presides over the world and to whom we are accountable, is holy, and He requires holiness in us. "Could not God," someone might ask, "be content to be holy Him-

self and leave us to our weakness and imperfection?" The
very asking of that question shows the difference between
God and us. God cannot be indifferent to moral imperfection for all unholiness is an attack upon His person and
nature. Therefore, God's holiness and its demands have been
revealed to us, first of all, in conscience. How mysterious
and wonderful is that voice that comes to us in the garden of
our soul, as it first came to fallen man in the garden, "Where
art thou?" This is a voice that cannot be evaded; it cannot be
bribed; it cannot be muffled or silenced. Conscience heaves
the soul as the tides heave the ocean.

Then God has revealed His holiness in His law which
He has given us in the Bible, and which is summarized in
the Ten Commandments. I once received a questionnaire
asking me to state which one of the Ten Commandments
I regarded as the most important. That would be impossible to do. All of the Commandments are equally against
sin and for God. The great purpose of the revealed law
was to teach the sinfulness of sin and the holiness of God.
Wherever that sense of God's holiness fades, the blight of
rejection of vital Christian truth and of lives conformed
to this world sets in. It was for this reason, no doubt, that
the first lesson those who were called to become the prophets, the spokesmen of God to mankind, had to learn was
that God is holy. When Moses saw the burning bush in
the desert, he hid his face. He was afraid to look upon
God who called to him out of the bush, "Put off thy shoes
from off thy feet, for the place whereon thou standest is
holy ground." When God spoke to Elijah in the wilder-
ness of Horeb, after the earthquake, the fire, and the
whirlwind, there came a still, small voice; Elijah wrapped
his face and went out and stood at the entrance of the
cave. When in the temple Isaiah saw the Lord sitting

upon a throne, high and lifted up, and His robe filling the temple, and heard the seraphim crying to one another, "Holy, holy, holy, is the Lord of Hosts," he said, "Woe is me! For I am undone; because I am a man of unclean lips, and I dwell in the midst of a people of unclean lips, for mine eyes have seen the King, the Lord of Hosts." When Jesus manifested Himself to Peter in the fishing boat, Peter fell down at His feet amid the nets and cried, "Depart from me, for I am a sinful man, O Lord." And when John saw the glory of Christ on Patmos, he fell at His feet as though dead. That is where the prophets and apostles commence, with the holiness of God. The song of Moses, through whom the law was given, is a song of holiness.

But this song of holiness is also the song of the Lamb. Paul tells us how the cross of Christ shows both the goodness and the severity of God. By the "severity of God," he means the requirements of God's holiness. "How," you ask, "does the cross show that?" By the offering up of Christ as the Lamb of God. Calvary, no less than Sinai, flames and flashes with the judgment of God against sin. The most overwhelming exhibition of what the holiness of God demands and what our sin deserves, is the death of Christ.

> Well might the sun in darkness hide,
> And shut his glories in,
> When Christ, the mighty Maker, died
> For man the creature's sin.

II. THE REDEMPTION OF GOD

The song of the Lamb strikes a second chord. The work of creation was followed by another work—the work of redemption from sin—a second creation, so to speak.

The saving of the world is a far greater feat than its creation out of nothing, great as that work was. The song of the Lamb is especially the melody of redemption. The law came by Moses; grace and truth came by Jesus Christ. The law could show holiness but not mercy. It could enlighten but not regenerate. It could tabulate results but not forgive. It could condemn but could not justify. The sacrifices of the Old Testament taught that an atonement, a satisfaction for sin, was necessary, because God is holy, "of purer eyes than to behold evil," and cannot acquiesce it. He must punish sin or in some other way render satisfaction to Himself. To solve this problem, God gave the world the Lamb of God. The demands of the broken law are met, not by us, but by Christ. He took my place and your place and bore our penalty so that justice was done and God remains just. Yet the same great act that does satisfaction to the law of God and restores the moral order also provides the way by which God can forgive sinners. Thus the song of the Lamb and the song of Moses is not only the song of God's holiness and justice on the throne but also of God's mercy and forgiveness. "There was a rainbow round about the throne." The throne of God's invincible justice and holiness stands forever, but it is circled about with the beautiful figure of speech when He says that He saw the Lamb standing in the midst of the throne. All-conquering, all-enduring, all-triumphant love is on the throne when the story of the universe has been summed up.

III. THE WAYS OF GOD

The third note in this great song is its ascription to the ways of God. "Just and true are thy ways, thou King of saints." In the opening lines of "Paradise Lost," John Milton tells us that his song is going to pursue "things unattempted yet in prose or rhyme," and asks the illumination of the Holy Spirit that he may "assert eternal providence and justify the ways of God to men." But that was too great a task for even the genius of John Milton. It takes the vision and the knowledge of those who stand there at the end of the ages upon the sea of glass mingled with fire to justify the ways of God to men.

The ways of God are often mysterious. "His way is on the sea," that is, there is something inscrutable and unfathomable in God's ways. The human intelligence cannot always follow the course of God's ways and His divine judgments. Here, in time and in this world, we can dimly discern that there is a principle of judgment at work. But there is much to perplex us. Some are punished now, while the punishment of others, often apparently more guilty, is deferred. "The sins of some are evident, going before them to judgment, while the sins of others follow after them." Often to our imperfect view, the evil nation or cause triumphs while the good goes down in what seems to be defeat and ruin. Evil appears to have the upper hand. Although here and there we catch the notes of a few beautiful voices—tender-toned, star-like, and clear—nevertheless, on the whole, the chorus that rises from the world is a coarse, brutal, and sensual cacophony. Yet we are asked to reconcile this way of God with the character of a God of infinite righteousness and love.

Again, there is a question of the ultimate ways of God, His final judgments. These trouble us so that we almost shrink from considering them. A line must be drawn, but how and where? How will it be drawn between Christians who heard and believed and heathen who never heard and so never believed? How will it be drawn between two persons with striking differences in their environments and in the examples they saw around them? Both heard, and one believed but the other did not. Some ask how there could be this personal examination into the lives of uncounted billions of people who have come into our world and gone from it like the waves beating upon the shores of the ocean or like the leaves of the forest that burst forth in the springtime and vanish in the autumn.

Again, there are the ways of God in our own lives. How many things we encounter here that we cannot understand. Mysteries so deep, and neither prayers nor tears can throw light on them.

These are some of the questions we cannot answer. But here in this Book of Revelation we have the answer when the whole story is told. That answer is the song of Moses and the Lamb, "Just and true are thy ways." The close of the human drama leaves God upon the throne of righteousness. When we stand where those singers stood, then we shall know and understand what we can know now only by faith.

I talked recently with an honored minister of Christ whose brother had been killed in a highway accident. He did not grieve over it, for his brother was aged and weary and lonely. It seemed to him that God in His wise providence had reached down and removed his brother from the trouble to come. You may have experienced circumstances in your life in which you could not so readily acknowledge the wise providence of God, except by faith. But in the end, on that day when we shall as Jesus said, ask no questions, we shall all see the wisdom of His ways and recognize how all things have worked together for our good.

> I'll bless the hand that guided,
> I'll bless the heart that planned
> When throned where glory dwelleth
> In Immanuel's land.
> With mercy and with judgment
> My web of life He wove,
> And e'en the dews of sorrow
> Were lustered with His love.

The song of Moses that they sang on that sea of glass makes one think of the song that Moses and the Israelites sang after God had opened a way for them through the Red Sea, saving them from the hands of the Egyptians, and when the Israelites saw the Egyptians dead upon the seashore. That song commemorated one particular victory over the enemies of God. But this new song of Moses and the Lamb celebrates the victory of God in every age over the powers of darkness and His final victory that will bring the conflict between God and all His foes to a close forever. As Moses and the Israelites stood upon the shore of the Red Sea and saw God's great deliverance when Pharaoh and his chariots were swallowed up in the waters of the sea, so redeemed humanity, standing upon the sea of glass mingled with fire, shall see and commemorate the final victory over sin.

The world seems a long way off from that song now. Yet the music that commenced that starlit night when Christ was born at Bethlehem of Judea, when the shepherds heard the angels sing, "Glory to God in the highest," has never died away. By faith it is possible for you and me to sing the song of Moses and the Lamb; to rejoice in the holiness of God; to find our joy in doing His will; and to marvel at the love with which He loves us one by one and in Christ has shown us that He is the one on whom we can depend in every time of need. We can rejoice, too, in His judgments, knowing that His ways with us are ever for our good; that all evil things, persons, and systems must go down; and that righteousness shall completely and forever triumph in Christ, the Lamb of God slain from the foundation of the world.

The only time to learn this song is now in this life. If you do not learn it now, you cannot sing it hereafter. You cannot choose Christ and put yourself on His side after He comes in glory and judgment. Nor can you choose Him and His side after you go to Him through the gates of death. The time to learn to sing the song of the Lamb is now. Have you learned this song? Have you come to His cross, and there joined in the song of the redeemed, "He loved me and gave himself for me"?

9

The Followers of the Lamb

*These are they which follow the Lamb
whithersoever he goeth.* (Revelation 14:4)

To follow the Lamb of God wherever He goes is our
chief business as Christians in this life. It will also be
our occupation, our joy, and our exceeding great reward
in the life to come.

In these great pictures of the Lamb of God in the Apocalypse we have beheld Him as: the one who opens the
seven-sealed book of human history and destiny; the one
through whom His followers overcome the powers of darkness; the one who wins the victory over the dragon and
the beast; the one whose precious blood the robes of the
saints have been washed and made white; and the one
whose song is the music of heaven and whose love is the

light of heaven. But here we have something different. Here we have the relationship of believers to Him. They are described as those who "follow the Lamb whithersoever he goeth."

Sometimes we wonder, and rightly so, about heaven. What will it be like? What will our occupations be there? In this description of those who follow the Lamb of God, we have the highest and final description of heaven. Not its streets of gold, its gates of pearl, its ever-flowing river of life, its mighty walls garnished with all sorts of precious stones, its great white throne encircled by a rainbow. These do not give us the final description of the heavenly life. That is found here in our text where we are told that the triumphant believers follow the Lamb of God whithersoever He goeth.

On a Communion Sabbath, the thought of this relationship will be helpful to us. Although personal relationships, when they are wrong and perverted and poisoned, bring life's acutest misery and suffering, they are nevertheless the source and fountain of life's highest joy. They make life tolerable. So the highest thought of our relationship to Christ is not that of devotion to the church, sacred and beautiful though it is, or to a set of doctrines, sublime and true though these doctrines may be, but to the person of Christ. To follow Him is our duty here and our destiny hereafter.

To follow Christ as the Lamb of God is a high responsibility. As members of the church of Christ we are the professed followers of Christ and so represent Him to the world. In that respect our lives are "either a Bible or a libel." We cannot evade this responsibility. You remember that in the Garden of Gethsemane, Peter drew his sword and cut off the ear of Malchus, a servant of the high priest. At once Jesus rebuked Peter and putting forth His hand, healed the wound that Peter had inflicted. Alas, how many misrepresentations of the Savior by His professed followers must Jesus mend and heal!

A follower of the Lamb of God must relate His life to the customs and habits of the world. There are places where Christ certainly would not go, letters He certainly would not write, books He certainly would not read. When you go to such places, when you do such things, can you truly say you are following Him? Then there are the things of the spirit. In your words, in your thoughts, in your attitudes, can you say that you are following Christ? The things of the spirit are deeper than the external things of life. John and James were, in many respects, loyal and faithful followers of Christ and devoted to His cause. When they wanted to call down fire upon a Samaritan village because it refused hospitality to Jesus, however, He rebuked them and told them they did know what spirit they were of. The Son of Man had come not to destroy life, He said, but to save it. Our goal, therefore, is to bring everything, even every thought, into captivity to Christ.

The task of following the Lamb of God has never been easy. It is not easy today. It has never been popular. It is not popular today. Still He says to His followers, "Strait is the gate, and narrow is the way, which leadeth unto life, and few there be that find it." This world was never a friend to grace. In certain respects it is more pagan, more alienated from God today than it was when those first disciples had to walk in it. This is the real test of the Christian life: following the Lamb of God *whithersoever* He goeth. Sometimes He leads us into hard and difficult places, and we have to make the decision whether or not to follow Him. Sometimes He leads us where "Eden's bowers bloom," but sometimes "mid scenes of deepest gloom." Sometimes by "waters calm," but sometimes "o'er troubled seas." That is the test. Will we follow Him when the way is hard? In a Pennsylvania churchyard, I read the epitaph of a godly minister written by himself:

> I have been eighty years
> In the service of Christ,
> Sixty as a minister:
> With him in evil report
> In sorrow and in joy.
> I leave my dying testimony—
> He was a Good Master!

Here was one who followed the Lamb of God through good and ill, in sunny days and in dark, through sorrow and through joy.

There is no joy, no reward, comparable to that of following the Lamb of God. That applies, first of all, to following Him in this life. To do this is to know the incomparable reward of conscience, whose "well done" is the highest decoration we can receive. To follow Him is to know the joy of giving, to learn how much more blessed it is to give than to receive. To follow Him is to know the joy of fighting for the only cause that will endure and conquer. To follow Him is to know the joy of Christian love and forgiveness, of ridding the heart of all sentiments of envy and hatred and anger and revenge. That is what Jesus meant when He said, "He that followeth me shall not walk in darkness."

Look for a moment at the traits and characteristics of this company who stood with the triumphant Lamb of God upon Mt. Zion. In the first place, they had their

Father's name written in their foreheads. Those who followed the world are spoken of as having the mark of the beast upon them, but the followers of Christ have His mark upon them. They are the open and public and confessed followers of Christ. No one can be a true follower of Christ and not come out publicly and confess it. Again, they are pure in their life, undefiled by the world. Jesus said, "Blessed are the pure in heart, for they shall see God." But how shall anyone's heart be pure unless it is cleansed by the Lamb of God Himself? Again, they are separated from the world for they have been "redeemed from among men," bought out of the captivity of this world. Again, they are loyal to Jesus in that they follow Him whithersoever He goeth. John also says of them, "In their mouth was found no guile." They are without deceit or dishonesty, clothed in the garments of integrity. Finally, they sing a "new song" of triumph that no others can sing, for unbelievers do not know this song. The song of Christian hope and faith and triumph can be sung only by those who know the Lord and love Him.

If to follow Christ is our joy and reward here, it certainly will be so hereafter. This is the crowning joy and satisfaction of the life to come. When we think of our loved ones and our friends who are now within the veil, what greater comfort could there be than to think of them as following the Lamb of God? "The Lamb which is in the midst of the throne shall feed them, and shall lead them unto living fountains of waters, and God shall wipe away all tears from their eyes." They understand now the full meaning of the twenty-third Psalm, "The Lord is my shepherd; I shall not want."

May God give His grace to you who are members of the church, who have written your names down, and who are on record as followers of the Lamb, so that you shall ever be able to choose Him before self and before this world. If some of you here today do not bear publicly the mark of Christ upon your brow, may God by his Holy Spirit bring you into the fellowship of those who follow the Lamb of God whithersoever He goeth. After all, who else is worthy of being followed? To whom in the straits of life can you go but to Him?

In his life of the celebrated English preacher, Arthur Penrhyn Stanley, the noted Dean of Westminster Abbey, Prothero relates the following incident:

A gentleman traveling in a third-class compartment from Norwich to Liverlpool fell into conversation with two soldiers from Chester. When he told them that he, too, was from a cathedral city, the city of Norwich, their faces lighted up as they exclaimed, "Why, that is where Dean Stanley lived!" When he asked them what they knew about Dean Stanley, one of them answered, "I and my companion here have cause to bless the Lord that we saw Dean Stanley."

He then told how when on leave in London, they spent the day sight-seeing. Late in the afternoon they came to Westminster Abbey, just as the doors were being locked. They turned away with disappointed looks and words that were overheard by a gentleman who told them that if it was impossible for them to come back the next day, he would show them the Abbey himself. He got the keys from the beadle and took them through the venerable church, pointing out the objects of greatest interest. As they stood by the monument to one of Britain's great soldiers, he said to the two men, "You wear the uniform of Her Majesty, and I dare say you would like to do some heroic deed worthy of a monument like this?" The soldiers both answered that they would. Then, laying a hand on each one of them, their guide said, "My friends, you may both have a more enduring monument than this for this will molder into dust and be forgotten; but if your names are written in the Lamb's Book of Life, you will abide forever."

As they were leaving the Abbey, their guide told them that he was the dean of the Abbey. The soldiers did not understand what he meant when he told them that if their names were written in the Lamb's Book of Life, they would abide forever. But in the course of time they came to know what he meant. They told the man in the railroad compartment with whom they had been talking, "We trust that our names are written in that Book of Life, and that in some way in God's own time we shall meet Dean Stanley in heaven."

All other attainments and achievements will finally fade and wither and crumble into dust, but if your name is written in the Lamb's Book of Life, you will abide forever. And forever you will join the company of His redeemed who follow the Lamb of God withersoever He goeth.

Part Two

The Secret of the Universe

Glory Be to Jesus

Glory be to Jesus,
 Who, in bitter pains,
Poured for me the life-blood
 From his sacred veins.
Grace and life eternal
 In that blood I find;
Blest be his compassion
 Infinitely kind.
Blest through endless ages
 Be the precious stream,
Which from endless torment
 Did the world redeem.
Abel's blood for vengeance
 Pleaded to the skies;
But the blood of Jesus
 For our pardon cries.
Oft as it is sprinkled
 On our guilty hearts,
Satan in confusion
 Terror-struck departs.
Oft as earth exulting
 Wafts its praise on high,
Angel-hosts rejoicing
 Make their glad reply.
Lift ye then your voices;
 Swell the mighty flood;
Louder still and louder
 Praise the precious blood!

Italian, c.1815; translated by Edward Caswall, 1857

10

The Blood of Christ: How It Cleanses

The blood of Jesus Christ, his Son cleanseth us from all sin. (1 John 1:7)

The ancient legend of the Holy Grail tells how Joseph of Arimathea, who got permission from Pilate to take the body of Jesus down from the cross and bury it, caught in a golden cup that Christ had held at the Last Supper the blood that flowed from the wound in His side. This he carried to Glastonbury on an island in Somerset in England. There he formed an order of knights whose work it was to protect the precious blood. The chief of these knights was made their king. When at certain times the king unveiled the golden cup that held the precious blood, a glorious and radiant light fell on the faces of all who stood about, filled them with rapture, and endued them with strength from on high. Only the pure in heart could look upon the cup and behold the wondrous light that streamed from the precious blood.

This beautiful story has played a great part in the history of our race. But there is one respect in which it stands in sharp contrast to the blood of Christ, as it is presented to us in the Gospels. Only the pure in heart, according to the legend of the Holy Grail, could look upon the precious blood. But the thing that the New Testament emphasizes about the blood of Christ is that it alone cleanses the stained and sinful heart.

The great apostle of love and of light tells us that "the blood of Jesus Christ his Son cleanseth us from all sin." Here we have the secret at the heart of the universe. The blood of Christ is the most powerful expression that the New Testament uses to represent the work of redemption that Christ did on the cross. This is the secret that Paul declared was hid from the beginning of the world and then was made known to the inhabitants and the powers of heaven and earth. It is the great secret of how God redeems mankind.

The blood of Christ, therefore, stands for the greatest thought and purpose of God, the greatest idea that the human mind can conceive, the greatest fact, past, present, and future. It is the eternal fact and the eternal act of redemption. Sometimes when we look out over the world and listen to its uproar and its confusion, when we see its deep and apparently unhealable wounds, when we behold its shame and its sin and defilement, when we listen to its cries of anguish and of woe, and when we see its malignant enmity to God and to righteousness, we almost despair of the future. The thing that gives us heart and hope and a rock upon which to stand is the fact that there is Another besides man at work in this world, that a higher wisdom is working out its eternal purpose, that on the cross God in Christ did a work that can never be undone, and that in God's own time will reconcile the world to Himself and bring in a kingdom of universal joy and peace.

In connection with the work that Christ did on the cross, the New Testament always presents to us two features or aspects of that work: first, how it delivers us from the penalty of sin; and second, how it cleanses us from the stain of sin. Sin always does these two things to us. It condemns us and it stains us. In logical sequence, we ought to speak first of how the blood of Christ pardons, and then how it washes away the stain of sin. But tonight we commence with this second great fact about the cross of Christ, that what was done there takes away the stain of sin.

I. THE STAIN OF SIN

This is frequently alluded to in the New Testament in connection with the blood of Christ. If you go through the New Testament after the four Gospels, you will find that the redeeming work of Christ is spoken of most frequently as the blood of Christ. This expression is used much more frequently than the cross, because it was what Christ did on the cross and what happened to Him there that counts for our salvation. So we are told that the blood of Christ cleanses us from all sin, that the redeemed in heaven have washed their robes and made them white in the blood of the Lamb, that the blood of Christ purges and cleanses our conscience, and that the redeemed in their songs around the throne of God praise Christ as the

One who loved them and washed them from their sins in His own blood.

There is no doubt about the stain of sin, and no doubt about the only power that can take away that stain. What is the stain of sin? It is partly the sense of guilt, the sense of having offended a holy and a just God. But together with that, there is an intense feeling that the soul has been defiled and left with a dark mark on it. I look everywhere in the world around me and, behold, everywhere I come across that dark mark of sin.

A young man of fine appearance, good reputation, and favorable position went to see his minister. In a few brief words, he disclosed the fact that his soul was scarred and stained by a sin that no one would ever have associated with him. The world's greatest need is not learning, not education, not physical health, but spiritual cleansing. This is what the blood of Christ proposes to do for us.

II. How the Blood of Christ Cleanses from Sin

The greatest of all miracles, the grandest of all facts is that the blood of Christ takes away, washes out, hides, covers, obliterates the stain of sin and the consciousness of that stain. "Though your sins be as scarlet, they shall be as white as snow; though they be red like crimson, they shall be as wool."

We are dealing here with something greater than we can define. But there is no question that this is the most wonderful of all realities. Nothing is more real than sin, and, thank God, nothing is more real than the experience of sin taken away by faith in a crucified Savior.

How the blood of Christ takes away our sins we can never know. We only know it was for us "he hung and

suffered there." But what we can know, what we are told
so plainly over and over again in the Bible is that on the
ground of the shed blood of Christ, God is pleased to
pardon all our sins. The announcement of this great fact
was prepared for in the Old Testament by the rituals of
sacrifice. In the law that God gave to Israel He said that
the people were not to partake of the blood, "for the life
of the flesh is in the blood, and I have given it to you
upon the altar to make an atonement for your souls, for it
is the blood that maketh an atonement for the soul." That
was the preparation for the great act of God on the cross.
The New Testament does not speak of the blood of Christ
as a thing apart and by itself, but as signifying and sym-
bolizing Christ's complete offering of Himself for our
sins on the cross. All that we can do is to bow down
before this sublime act and exclaim, "Even so, Lord, for
so it pleaseth thee."

The blood of Christ delivers us from the stain of sin
because it assures us of the love of God. Somewhere in a
cathedral in England over their graves are the effigies of a
crusader knight and his lady. The exquisite effigy of the
lady, however, is without a right hand. According to tradition, in the wars of the Crusades, this knight was captured
by the Moslem conqueror, Saladin. The knight besought
Saladin to spare his life for the sake of the love that his lady
in England bore towards him, but Saladin scoffed and said
that she would soon forget him and marry another. When
the knight insisted that she would never do that, Saladin
asked for a proof. He added that if the lady sent him her
right hand, he would release the knight from the sentence
of death. A letter was sent to the lady in England, who
promptly had her right hand cut off and sent it to the
Moslem conqueror. When Saladin saw it he set the knight

free and sent him back to England. The severed hand was
the proof of that woman's great love. So the blood of Christ,
which was shed for our redemption, is the proof that God
loves us. That knowledge give us hope.

III. Only the Blood of Christ Can Cleanse from Sin

Sin is the most dreadful fact in the universe. Do not be
offended, therefore, when the Bible tells us that God deals
with sin in blood. There were no silver mists or rosy
sunsets about the cross. The crown of thorns, the spear
thrust into Christ's side, the nails that the Roman soldiers
drove through His flesh—remember, these were not figures of speech; they were terrible realities. So also was the
blood of Christ. It is by that reality that our sins are taken
away and in no other way.

I can imagine a great convocation in heaven when God
announced to its inhabitants that His human creatures
had fallen and His new creation was now stained with sin.
From every quarter of the universe, the great angels come
posting in, riding upon the wings of the wind, to hear the
dread announcement by the Almighty. When God asks
for a remedy and calls for volunteers to go down to earth
and deliver human beings from the curse of sin, one great
angel comes forward and says, "I will go down to earth. I
will live a life of peace and truth and purity and love
before them, and by this I mean I will win their souls to
the good. Thus I will take away the stain of sin."

But God answers, "Your way of life is good, but it will
not turn them from their sin, neither can it take away the
stain of their sin."

Then another angel comes forward and says, "I will go
down. I will teach the truth to human beings. I will fill

their minds with the precepts of righteousness, and thus contemplating the truth, they shall be delivered from the stain of sin."

But again the Almighty answers, "Your precepts are good, and your statutes are right, but they cannot deliver human beings from sin or wash away the stain of sin. They will only remind them of what they have lost and whence they have fallen. Your precepts are efficient, but not sufficient."

Then a third angel comes forward and says, "I will go down to earth and I will tell them of a great hope. I will lure them out of their sins by the music of the hope of a future life that shall be sinless. Thus they shall arise and follow after righteousness, and thus they shall lose the stain of their sin."

But once more God answers, "Mighty spirit, sweet is the music of hope, but the hope about which you will sing to human beings cannot save them. It will only sadden their hearts with the difference between what they are and what you tell them they may become."

For a time, there was silence in heaven. Then the Son of God, in whose face was the brightness of the Father's glory, and before whom the angels and archangels, the cherubim and seraphim, bowed down in reverence, came and spoke, "Eternal Father, I will go down. By the power of the Holy Spirit, I will take human nature upon myself. By the power of the eternal Spirit, I will offer myself on the cross and shed my precious blood. My blood will cleanse them from their sin." All the hosts of heaven rejoiced at these words and cried together with a voice like the sound of many waters, "Eternal Son, go down! You only can redeem fallen human beings. Your blood alone will cleanse them from their sin."

Yes, this is the only remedy for sin. This is the heart of the Gospel. And the heart of the Gospel is the secret at the heart of the universe. All of us need this cleansing. Not only once, but always, day after day, week after week. Let us come to this fountain that we may be cleansed from all our sins.

Once I received a letter asking, "Can Christ do anything for my sin?" The question told of the struggle of a soul that had sinned specifically and was reaching out for Christ as a drowning person reaches out for a life preserver. Uppermost in the mind of the writer was the stain of sin.

Can Christ do anything for our sin? Yes, Christ can do something. Indeed, He can do everything that needs to be done for our sin. For "the blood of Jesus Christ his Son cleanseth us from all sin."

11

The Blood of Christ: How It Reconciles

In whom we have redemption through his blood. (Ephesians 1:7)

It is a bright December day in 1859, at Charlestown, Virginia, in the beautiful Valley of Shenandoah, the daughter of the stars. A crowd has gathered on the street in front of a brick building. Soldiers with fixed bayonets keep the crowd back. The door opens and a man is led down the steps. He is dressed in a black frock coat, and on his feet are red carpet slippers. Before he gets into the wagon to be driven to the scaffold, where he is to be hanged by the neck until dead, John Brown hands to one of the guards a bit of paper. It is his last message to the world. "I, John Brown, am now quite certain that the crimes of this guilty land will never be purged away but with blood."

Everybody in the South said that John Brown died as the murderer dies, and the great majority of people in the North said that he died as the fool dies. But wisdom was justified of her children. 1860, 1861, 1862—just three years and the ground on which John Brown's scaffold stood was shaking and quaking to the thunder of the artillery firing across the Potomac on the banks of the Little Antietam. On the 17th of September, the bloodiest day of the Civil War, John Brown's prophecy of an atonement of blood came true. The nation was preserved, the sin of slavery was washed away, but not without the shedding of blood.

In his prophetic message, John Brown gave expression to a truth that has a deeper and wider significance than the illustrations of it in the history of nations. That is, the truth of the Scriptures, the great secret of redemption, that without the shedding of blood, the precious blood of Christ, there is no remission of sins.

Two conceptions of Christianity are abroad in the world today. Or, more correctly, we might say that there is a true Christianity and there is a false Christianity that merely wears the name. According to the false conception, Christianity is a religion of conduct. It centers upon what we can do or ought to do, as we are instructed, inspired, and led by the teachings, the example, and the tragic death of Jesus. According to the true conception, Christianity is a religion of redemption from sin. It centers upon what Christ did on the cross, when He offered Himself as an atoning sacrifice for our sins.

The scholarly and cultivated son of a Chinese Christian pastor recently wrote an article under the heading, "I Am A Pagan." He declares that he has renounced Christianity, and as a proof of that renunciation, he says that he has abandoned the idea of redemption. This Chinese man was sensible enough and frank enough to confess that when you have abandoned the idea of redemption, you have abandoned Christianity. You may keep the Christian name, you may cling to the Christian virtues, but when you give up redemption, you have given up Christianity. Likewise, the person who in experience has never arrived at the idea of redemption has never yet arrived at Christianity.

The secret at the heart of the world is redemption from sin, and the secret of redemption is the blood of Christ. So Paul writes, "In whom we have redemption through his blood, the forgiveness of sins, according to the riches of his grace." The crimson line of blood can be traced across every page of the Bible. We see it in the sacrifices of the patriarchs, in the covenants that God made with His people, in the worship of the tabernacle and the temple, in the predictions of the prophets, in the words of Jesus, in the teachings of the apostles, and in the hymns and songs of the redeemed in heaven.

The death of Christ, and that is what the New Testament means by the blood of Christ, is God's plan to redeem the world. The Scriptures present sin under two aspects: the aspect of guilt or condemnation and the aspect of stain. Sin always does these two things to us: it condemns us and it stains us. Likewise, the Scriptures tell of two effects of the blood of Christ: it takes away our guilt and it takes away the stain of our sin. As St. John put it, "The blood of Jesus Christ his Son cleanseth us from all sin." Previously we spoke of this second effect of the blood of Christ, how it cleanses us from sin. Now we shall speak of that which logically comes first, how the blood of Christ takes away the guilt and the penalty of our sin.

I. SIN LEAVES US GUILTY AND CONDEMNED

Here we are dealing with the most solemn thing in the world, the law of God. The Scriptures testify that all people have sinned, that the wages of sin is death, and that the soul that sins shall die. This is a fact of God's universe. It is a fact that is in no way changed because we may not feel guilty or condemned. As Coleridge once put it, the two great poverties of our day are the poverty of the lack of the sense of God and the poverty of the lack of the sense of sin.

What the Bible teaches is confirmed by human experience and by the human conscience. Conscience tells us that we have broken the law of God. Not our own law, not the law of someone else, but a higher law; that is, the law of God. There can be no doubt that our sin separates us and alienates us from God. When one man has wronged another or has spoken falsely or unkindly about him, he generally avoids that man. So we have sought to avoid God. Sin always drives people away—our first parents from the Garden of Eden, Jacob from his father's house, Judas from the Lord's Supper, Peter from the presence of the Lord. The history of the world, the history of the human heart shows that the whole world lies in sin and under condemnation. Our sin is written with a pen of iron and with the point of a diamond. Sin is the one great calamity. It is as universal as human nature, as enduring as human history.

II. HOW THE BLOOD OF CHRIST RECONCILES AND REDEEMS US

What a great and beautiful thing it is when someone reconciles those who have been enemies and makes them friends. Both Martin Luther and John Bunyan brought their great lives to a close in attempts to reconcile men: Luther, two brothers; Bunyan, a father and a son. But how much greater and how much more beautiful is God's act of reconciling sinners to Himself by the precious blood of Christ. The Gospel declares that we are reconciled to God by the death of Christ on the cross. All that this means perhaps we can never know, but we do know that this is God's way, God's plan. Christ died for us, not in the general sense of benevolence, but He died in our stead; He died as our substitute. It pleased God to accept the righteousness and the sufferings of Christ as a complete satisfaction for our sins. At the cross all that the broken law required was done. The holiness and justice of God were upheld, while at the same time His infinite love was revealed. The penalty for sin was lifted from us because it was borne by Christ. Nothing less than this could satisfy God, and nothing less than this could satisfy us or bring peace to our souls.

There is an interesting story in the history of Scotland's great hero, Robert Bruce, the man whose heart Douglas flung before his troops as they rushed into battle against the English, exclaiming, "Brave heart, we will follow thee!" Pursued once by the English with bloodhounds, Bruce and his followers were in desperate straits. His companions had given up all hope of escape. But the courageous Bruce took them down into a small stream, walked with them for some distance in the waters up the bed of the stream, threw the dogs off their scent, and thus they escaped. So the retribution, penalty, and punishment that is our due was turned back in the crimson tide that flowed from Calvary's tree.

This indispensableness and the reasonableness of the

death of Christ becomes evident when we ask ourselves for what other reason would God have permitted His Son to die upon the cross. Even Christ in His human nature seems to have wondered if there was no other way, for in His agony in the Garden of Gethsemane He prayed, "If it be possible, let this cup pass from me." But although Jesus said, "With God all things are possible," here was one thing that was not possible even with God: that sin should be taken away and we should be redeemed except by the death of the Son of God.

Let us imagine that when the fall of man and the subject of redemption were first disclosed by God in the heavenly councils, that God asked the high intelligences of heaven to suggest some way of dealing with the great injury that sin had wrought to the universe and to human souls. One great spirit comes forward and says, "Eternal Father, thy creation is vast. The world is but a speck of dust, and human beings are only one of the hosts of created beings. Let us, therefore, overlook and ignore their sin. Let thy eternal heart rejoice in the adoration and praise of the unfallen multitudes." But the eternal Father answers, "Your plan does not honor my justice and my holiness, neither does it satisfy the yearnings of my heart."

Then another spirit comes forward and says, "Eternal Father, humans are weak; they have fallen and have been tempted and seduced by our great enemy. They have sinned against thy majesty and thy holiness. But show them thy mercy. Remit the penalty of death upon their sin. What plan is necessary, what measure is required, except the mere word of thy decree, 'You are forgiven'?"

But the eternal Father answers, "Your proposal of restoration without repentance, of redemption without reconciliation, or pardon without justice would dishonor the majesty of heaven. It would not heal the breach between sinful human beings and God, neither would it bestow peace upon their guilty hearts."

Then the divine Son comes forward and says, "Eternal Father, I will redeem, pardon, reconcile, and restore thy fallen children, but not at the expense of thy holiness and thy justice. I will assume their nature. In that nature, I will perfectly obey thy law. I will offer myself through the eternal Spirit on the cross. I will drink their cup of judgment for them. I will bear their penalty in my own body on the tree. I will die as their substitute."

Then all heaven rings with the adoring praise of the angels because of the love and the power of a crucified Savior.

That substitution on the cross died for you and for me. He is "the Lamb of God which taketh away the sin of the world." That is why every true church of Christ has that Lamb, as it were, carved in the stones of its walls.

12

The Blood of Christ: How It Conquers

And they overcame by the blood of the Lamb (Revelation 12.11)

When the seventh angel sounded, great voices were heard in heaven. The temple of God was opened to the accompaniment of lightnings, voices, thunderings, an earthquake, and great hail. Then appeared a great wonder, "a woman clothed with the sun, and the moon under her feet, and upon her head a crown of twelve stars." This woman clothed in incomparable glory has generally been taken to represent the church of Christ. Wherever the church appears in the Scriptures, she is radiant with majesty and glory. The magnificent description of the church here is in keeping with that in the Song of Solomon, "fair as the moon, clear as the sun, and terrible as an army with banners." But greater than the glory of the sun and the moon and the stars is that with which the apostle Paul clothes the church when he calls her "the body of Christ."

Over against this woman so beautifully arrayed appeared a dragon. As the woman is incomparable in her beauty, so the dragon is incomparable in his hideousness. He is a great red dragon, "having seven heads and ten horns, and seven crowns upon his heads." This description may mean that as the head of the kingdom of evil he has great power. The numerous heads and horns may indicate that there is diversity in his evil deeds, and that he is bound by no fixed laws or systems. With his tail he drew after him the third part of the stars of heaven. What a picture that is of fallen angels and fallen human beings, too. The stars of heaven fixed to the tail of the dragon. There we have the tragedy of those who were meant to be ligh-bearers dragged down from their heights to become the servants of evil.

The dragon waited before the woman to destroy the child to which she was soon to give birth. There we have a powerful picture of evil always at war with good, ever seeking to destroy the good at its very beginning, in its very first impulses. Wherever a good movement is established in the world, Satan seeks to corrupt it and pollute it. Wherever a church is built, the devil builds a chapel. Wherever a good purpose or aspiration or impulse appears in the hearts of people, Satan is there, ready to destroy it, if possible. The picture of the dragon waiting before the sun-clad woman to devour her child makes one think of Pharaoh trying to frustrate the plan of God by destroying the first-born in Egypt and Herod slaying the children in Bethlehem in order to slay the King of the Jews.

But the child was caught up into heaven safe out of the dragon's clutches, and the mother was miraculously protected from the dragon in the desert. Although he always makes war against it, Satan is never able to destroy the vital principle of truth and true religion. Always a faithful remnant is left.

Now the war that the dragon had been making against the woman and the church on earth broke out in heaven. Michael and his angels fought against the dragon and his angels. The dragon and his hosts were overcome and were cast out of heaven. Then John heard the song of victory and of triumph, "And I heard a loud voice saying in heaven, 'Now is come salvation and strength, and the kingdom of our God and the power of his Christ, for the accuser of our brethren is cast down, which accused them before our God day and night. And they overcame him by the blood of the Lamb and by the word of their testimony, and they loved not their lives unto the death. Therefore rejoice, ye heavens, and ye that dwell in them.'"

The Apocalypse is a book of flaming symbols. We need not trouble ourselves as to the objectivity of the things that are described in it. They may, indeed, have real literal existence. It would not be strange if there were real angels and real dragons and real war in heaven just as there are real men and real wars on earth. But underneath all this gorgeous and fearful phantasmagoria is the comforting and inspiring truth that in the war between good and evil, God is on the side of right and faith. Christ's cause and church, though embattled, shall be victorious. Christian believers, though they must ever fight, can overcome all their foes by the blood of the Lamb, that is, by the power of their faith in the crucified Son of God.

Thus far in this series of sermons, we have seen the

effect of the blood of Christ on our past sins: first, how it takes away the guilt and condemnation of our sin, justifying and pardoning and reconciling us to God; and second, how it washes away the stain of our sin. Now we are to see how in temptation it is our help, and how through the blood of Christ we conquer in our warfare with sin.

I. THE SOUL MUST FIGHT

There is no doubt about the conflict. There is no victory without a battle. "Sure I must fight if I would reign." Always there is a dragon ready to make war on the soul. In appearance, however, he is never a dragon but rather an angel of light. Satan has infinite disguises: sophistries, lies, and deceptions with which he endeavors to entrap and destroy the soul. This ancient foe is always waiting and watching for us.

Until the power of their enemy was finally broken, the pioneers on this western frontier did all their work and carried on all the activities of life conscious of the fact that a hostile eye was always watching them. Whether it was work in the field, rocking the cradle, or worship in the rude churches, they knew that that an enemy attack was always possible, always to be expected. So we Christians carry on all the activities of our life under the eye of our great enemy and God's. This is the meaning of Paul's exhortation, "Put on the whole armor of God, that ye may be able to stand against the wiles of the devil." This, too, is the meaning of Peter's warning, "Be sober, be vigilant because your adversary the devil, as a roaring lion, walketh about, seeking whom he may devour."

II. Victory by the Blood of the Lamb

In this great battle with the dragon and his angels described in the Apocalypse, the followers of Christ overcame their foes through the blood of the Lamb. What we have here, then, is the pictorial statement of the truth that the blood of the Atonement, the cross, touches hidden sources of power within the reach of every true believer.

Satan is vanquished by the blood of Christ. When through wicked men he secured the crucifixion of Christ, what seemed to be his greatest triumph was in reality his overthrow and his doom. For Satan's empire fell when Christ died on the cross. In the faith of the Cross multitudes of souls have overcome the evil one. The Jews have an old legend that Satan, who in this passage is represented as the accuser of the brethren of Christ, accuses the people of God on every day except the Day of Atonement. But before the blood of Christ, Satan is disarmed.

Martin Luther once had a dream in which he stood on the Day of Judgment before God. Satan was there to accuse him. When the books were opened, Satan pointed to transgression after transgression of which Luther was guilty. Luther's heart sank in despair. Then he remembered the Cross, and turning upon the devil he said, "There is one entry that you have not made." "What is that?" asked Satan. "It is this," answered Luther, "The blood of Jesus Christ his Son cleanseth us from all sin."

III. How the Blood of Christ Gives Us Victory Over Temptation and Sin

In the first place, the blood of Christ reveals the hideousness and the ugliness of sin and thus creates a hatred of it and a recoil from it. It is only as a pretended friend of the soul, as one who would give the soul high and secret joys, that temptation is able to do its work. But the blood of Christ, the thought of the Cross, removes the fair mask from the face of temptation, and we see sin in its true and terrible colors. We see that sin is so terrible that nothing less than the precious blood of Christ could atone for it. Satan is exposed in his true nature. No longer does he appear as an angel of light but as the father of lies. Although it has suffered great abuse, there is real spiritual meaning behind the old Catholic tradition about the devil fleeing before the sign of the cross. Those who most clearly and earnestly set before them Christ as the only Redeemer from sin are the ones who are most successful in their warfare with evil.

Again, the blood of Christ, the thought that Christ died and suffered for our sins, affords the highest motives for the Christian life. Emotions produced by the cross have no saving power; only the blood that was shed on the cross can save, justify, reconcile, and cleanse us. Yet the very meditation upon the fact affords a powerful motive for the Christian life. This undoubtedly is what Paul meant when he said that being reconciled by Christ's death, we shall be saved by His life. The living Christ who shed His blood for us on the cross has now become our leader and the Captain of our Salvation.

It is interesting that both Peter and John who were so much in the company of Jesus, who saw His miracles and heard His sermons, when they come to urge fidelity, patience, brotherly love, and endurance in the Christian life never mention any saying of Jesus as we would probably do, never mention any of His miracles, but refer only to His death on the cross. So when Peter encourages believers to be holy in everything they do; he reminds them that they were redeemed from a worldly life with the precious blood of Christ. When he exhorts them to fortitude in suffering, he recalls how Christ suffered on the cross and tells them to arm themselves with the same mind. When John appeals to Christian disciples to love one another, he quotes no beautiful saying of Jesus, as he might have done, but reminds them that Christ laid down His life for them on the cross; therefore, they ought to love one another.

Because of the words, "They loved not their lives unto the death" some have thought that this whole passage in Apocalypse from which our text is taken refers only to the martyrs and that they are the ones who overcame by the blood of the Lamb. But there is no reason to think that this great promise is for the martyrs alone. It is a promise of victory for all who trust in the crucified Savior. Nevertheless, it is wondrously true that the martyrs did overcome by the blood of Christ. Stretched on the rack, nailed to a cross, standing on the brink of a precipice, bound to the stake with the fagots crackling about them, or thrown into the arena to the wild beasts, they loved not their lives unto the death. They made a glorious confession because in their hour of suffering they thought of Christ on Calvary suffering for their redemption and armed themselves with the same mind. Call the long roll of the martyrs. Invoke the whole company of the blood-besprinkled throng and ask them how they overcame. Their answer is always the same, "We overcame through the blood of the Lamb."

Give me the wings of faith to rise
Within the veil, and see

The saints above, how great their joys,
How bright their glories be.
I ask them whence their victory came;
They, with united breath,
Ascribe their conquest to the Lamb,
Their triumph to His death.

The blood of Christ is to us all the sign of the final victory: His victory, our victory, and the victory of all the brethren of Christ. By this sign conquer! There is an immense encouragement for every one of us in the shed blood of the cross. It tells us that we, too, shall one day be conquerors and more than conquerors through Him who loved us and gave Himself for us.

13

The Resurrection and the Cross

Now the God of peace, that brought again from the dead our Lord Jesus, that great shepherd of the sheep, through the blood of the everlasting covenant, make you perfect in every good work to do his will, working in you that which is well–pleasing in his sight, through Jesus Christ, to whom be glory for ever and ever, Amen. (Hebrews 13:20–21)

Some years ago a popular English novelist wrote a book called *When It Was Dark*. The story centers about the efforts of a wealthy unbeliever to discredit Christianity. He endeavors to do this by attempting to discredit the resurrection of Christ. In this respect his logic is sound, for if the resurrection can be discredited, Christianity is overthrown. The man hired venal archeologists to fake a discovery of the body of Jesus in a tomb in the neighborhood of Jerusalem. On the tomb was an inscription testifying that the owner of this sepulchre stole the body of Jesus and hid it there. The novel then goes on to describe the ultimate effect such a discovery, if accepted as truth, would have upon the Christian world, the Christian church, and civilization in general. In powerful passages he shows how the Christian church gradually crumbles and collapses. Men and women go back to lust, cruelty, and animalism, and the flame of hope dies out in every human heart.

Had the body of Christ ever been found or had a grave been found other than the grave of Joseph of Arimathea where it could be proved that the body of Christ had been placed, the church would indeed disappear, and the sun of human hope would set in the darkness of never-ending despair. But thanks be to God, now is Christ risen from the dead! On that empty tomb is the epitaph written by the angels, the epitaph that ends all other epitaphs, "He is risen; he is not here; behold the place where they laid him."

People have tried to imagine what the world would be like if Christ had not come. In our imagination we might consider another question, "What would the world be like if Christ had not risen from the dead?" The difference would be just the same as if Christ had not been born and had not died. "But why would this be so?" one might ask. "Even if Jesus had not risen, would we still not have the story of the incarnation? The choral chant of the angels? The miracles of mercy? The parables of wisdom? The Sermon on the Mount? The beauty of Christ's life and example and the pathos of his unmerited death? Would we still not have all this, even if Christ had not risen from the dead?" The answer is, "No!" All would have perished in that grave from which Jesus never returned. Matthew Arnold's terrible lines would sum up the story of our Lord:

> Now he is dead; far hence he lies
> In that lorn Syrian town;
> And on his grave with shining eyes
> The Syrian stars look down.

The disciples preached Christ and the Resurrection, that is, Christ as the Son of God, our King and Lord, our Savior by His death on the cross, our Prince and Ruler who is to come, all sealed and confirmed by the great act of God in the resurrection. So Peter in his sermon at Pentecost, the first great Christian sermon, devotes most of the sermon to the Resurrection as proof that the crucified Jesus is both Lord and Christ, and that by the Resurrection God exalted Jesus to be a Prince and Savior to give repentance to Israel and the forgiveness of sins. The Cross is the central and saving fact of Christianity, but the foundation fact—that which upholds all the rest—is the Resurrection.

I. THE PURPOSE OF THE CROSS

In this text from the Letter to the Hebrews, we have one of the great passages on the Resurrection, "The God of peace, that brought again from the dead our Lord Jesus, . . . through the blood of the everlasting covenant . . ." This comes at the end of a book in which the major note is Christ's atonement for sin. All through this letter a parallel is drawn to the Old Testament sacrifices. As the high priest once each year on the great Day of Atonement went within the veil of the tabernacle to sprinkle the mercy seat with the blood of a lamb as an atonement for the sins of the people, so Christ, who is both the Victim and the High Priest, offered Himself once and for all on the cross, and with His own blood He has gone within the veil of heaven itself to make atonement and intercession for us. The other covenants that God made with man were temporary, prophetic of the everlasting covenant that He made in Christ and that was sealed with the blood of Christ.

The author of Hebrews makes the bold and unusual statement that God raised up Christ by the blood of the everlasting covenant, that is, by virtue of His death on the cross for our sins. Death is the wages of sin and our last enemy. By taking the full penalty of our sins upon Himself and therefore tasting death for us, Christ overcame death and destroyed its power.

II. THE IMPORTANCE OF THE RESURRECTION

Thus the Resurrection is said to be God's great witness to the saving and redeeming power of the death of Christ. The Resurrection has meaning only in connection with what Christ did on the cross. Suppose for a moment that we were told that Christ died and rose again, but nothing was said about the purpose of His death. The resurrection would then be an astounding prodigy, but nothing more— related to nothing else and teaching us nothing at all. As the final act in the redeeming work of Christ, however, it has immense and indispensable and immeasurable meaning. It tells us that the work of redemption has been accomplished and salvation made possible for everyone. What we commemorate in the Resurrection, then, is not only the resurrection of Christ Himself, or His resurrection as a prophecy of our own resurrection, but the whole length and breadth and height of Christianity, the whole faith once delivered to the saints.

Included in that are the great truths: that God is our Creator and Father, who never leaves Himself without a witness in the world; that Jesus is the very Son of God, declared by the Resurrection to be both Lord and Christ; that human beings are immortal, created in the image of God with free will, yet in revolt against God and fallen from their high estate; that God so loved the world that in the incarnation He sent His Son, Jesus Christ, to seek and to save the lost; that Christ saves us by His death; that a glorious destiny awaits believers, who will be changed into the likeness of Christ in His risen glory; and that truth and righteousness and peace shall at last reign supreme and forever. These are the glorious truths we celebrate in the resurrection of Jesus. How great and precious they are! They represent the highest spiritual treasures of mankind. Let us rejoice that they stand supported and buttressed by nothing less powerful than the resurrection of Jesus Christ from the dead!

How desperately our broken, staggering, unresting, suspicious, embittered world needs the comfort and the inspiration of these great Christian truths. Nothing else will keep us from plunging into the abyss—not science, nor education, nor culture, nor political organization, but only the grand hopes and facts of the Christian faith to which the Resurrection bears its glorious and invincible witness.

The Bible is able, always, to relate the sublimest truths to the needs of our daily life. So the writer of this noble passage on the Atonement and the Resurrection says, "Now the God of peace, that brought again from the

dead our Lord Jesus, that great shepherd of the sheep, through the blood of the everlasting covenant, make you perfect in his sight, through Jesus Christ, to whom be glory for ever and ever." How wonderful this is! Christ's death on the cross and His resurrection from the dead provide you and me in our daily life—our daily struggles, our sorrows, and our temptations—with the power we need to do the will of God, who through Christ is working in us His own eternal purposes. Therefore, let us lift up our hearts. Resurrection Day gives us the assurance that our sins are forgiven through the blood of the everlasting covenant, that we can do the will of God in our lives every day, and that when this life is over a glorious immortality awaits us beyond the grave.

Scripture Text Index

Other Clarence E. Macartney Sermon Books

Chariots of Fire

Drawing upon colorful yet lesser-known characters of the Old and New Testaments, Dr. Clarence Macartney presents eighteen powerful and timeless sermons. One of America's greatest biographical preachers, Macartney aims for the common heart of human experience. Each sermon contains a wealth of illustrations and quotations that add depth and insight to the exposition. *Chariots of Fire* is eye-opening, biblical exposition from one of America's premier preachers and makes an inspiring devotional or study resource.

ISBN 0-8254-3274-x   192 pages   paperback

Great Women of the Bible

A collection of sermons from a master pulpiteer of yesterday. Macartney's unique descriptive style brings these women of the Bible to life and provides inspirational reading for all Christians.

ISBN 0-8254-3268-5   208 pages   paperback

Greatest Texts of the Bible

This collection of sermons represents some of the author's strongest and most impassioned preaching. Except for slight modifications and updating, and the insertion of Scripture references where needed, these sermons are reissued in their original form.

ISBN 0-8254-3266-9   208 pages   paperback

He Chose Twelve
This careful study of the New Testament illuminates the personality and individuality of each of the Twelve Disciples. A carefully crafted series of Bible character sketches including chapters on all the apostles as well as Paul and John the Baptist.

ISBN 0-8254-3270-7   176 pages   paperback

Paul the Man
Macartney delves deeply into Paul's background and heritage, helping twentieth-century Christians understand what made him the pivotal figure of New Testament history. Paul's career as missionary and theologian is carefully traced in this insightful work.

ISBN 0-8254-3269-3   208 pages   paperback

Strange Texts But Grand Truths
Drawing upon seventeen striking and unusual texts of Scripture, Macartney utilizes the natural curiosity aroused by the unfamiliar to expound the important and practical truths of God's Word. Macartney brings to life overlooked lessons from biblical passages. Each sermon contains a wealth of illustrations and quotations that add depth and insight to the exposition of one of America's premier preachers, making this volume an inspiring devotional or study resource.

ISBN 0-8254-3272-3   192 pages   paperback

Twelve Great Questions About Christ
Macartney addresses commonly asked questions about the life and person of Jesus Christ. The integrity of the Scriptures underlies the provocative answers that Dr. Macartney provides in this thoughtful book. The broad range of subject matter will inform and inspire laymen and clergy.

ISBN 0-8254-3267-7   160 pages   paperback